KNOWING GOD PERSONALLY

BY

TERRY A. ANDERSON

New Life Publishing
PO Box 747
Burnet, Texas 78611
USA

NEW LIFE PUBLISHING

Published in the United States of America by New Life
Publishing, Burnet, Texas, 78611 (www.fellowshipalive.com).

ISBN 0-9678900-0-4

Printed in the United States of America

TO THE BRIDE OF CHRIST
TO THOSE WHO ARE ALIVE IN HIM

Contents

Preface   7

Section I
PEACE THROUGH RELATIONSHIP   9
The Path To Personal Peace   11

1. Pathways of Life   11
2. Journey to Self-Identity   14
3. Pausing to Observe the Meaning of Life   19
4. The Pathway to Freedom   23
5. Passing through the Battle   28
6. The Path from Fear to Courage   33
7. Going through Suffering to Blessing   39
8. Fellowship on the Path   44
9. Staying on the Path   48
10. Living in Peace   52
11. Come on Home   56

Section II
GOING ON TO JOY   59
Joy Out of Sorrow and Pain   59

1. Happiness or Joy   61
2. How Shall We React To Sorrow and Pain?   63
3. If Our Hearts Make us Feel Guilty   65
4. Wiping The Slate Clean   67
5. New Life From God   70
6. Sorrow, Pain and the Fruit called Joy   72

Section III
GOING ON TO LOVE
WITHOUT FEAR   73
Fearless Love   73

1. The Purpose of Life   74
2. What are Personal Relationships?   77
3. The Cycle of Fear   79
4. The Cycle of Fearless Love   81
5. An Anchor of Love   82
6. Getting to Know God   84
7. We Must Open the Door   87

Section IV
GOING THROUGH HINDRANCE
TO VICTORY   91

Receiving God's Love   92

1.	Human Love or God's Love	92
2.	Accepting from Others	94
3.	Abiding in the Vine	96
4.	Humility	97
5.	Controlling the Ego	98
6.	An Exchange of Love	101

Section V
GOING ON TO THE
ABUNDANCE IN LIFE   102

Living More Abundantly   102

1.	Receiving From God	106
2.	Personal Relationships	109
3.	Spirit-Filled Abundance	111
4.	Commanded to Love	114
5.	The Key To Loving God	117
6.	Abundance Means Much Fruit	119
7.	Normal Christian Life	124

PREFACE

John Bunyan, who wrote *The Pilgrams Progress* in the latter part of the 17th century, portrayed the Christian life as exactly what it is - a journey. For many years I did not understand that my salvation was only a beginning - that if I was going to live the Christian life, I must journey from salvation to friendship with my Lord (John 15:15 & 16). I did not know that I needed to know Him personally - the journey, for me, had not even begun.

As I later thought about this great old classic called *The Pilgrams Progress*, I began my journey. I began to read the scripture in a search for a personal relationship with God. The more I read, the more I realized that this is what the whole Bible is about. From Genesis to Revelation and especially the teaching of Jesus in the Gospels; the underlying message is that God loves us and earnestly desires that we love Him and fellowship with Him. I also realized that we seldom trust someone we do not know and that the way to trust God is through a close personal relationship with Him. More and more I am realizing that this relationship is the pathway in a journey to peace, joy, fearlessness and all the abundance of God's grace.

I did not think I would ever write about this journey in a such a detailed way because none of us have "arrived" - at best, we are on the pathway to more and more fellowship with our Lord. What you are about to read is a compilation of a series of articles that I have written and later drawn together to form a complete volume on the subject of knowing God personally in a world that is characterized by sorrow and pain.

I believe that, as you read through these pages, you will become more aware of the reasons that, next to salvation, a personal relationship with God is the most valuable thing we can ever possess. If your journey has not begun or if you have turned aside, I hope you will join me on the pathway. I will be sharing with you the things the Holy Spirit has shown me thus far. As you tread this pathway I hope He will show you any other things you may need in your life and things you can share with others (we are all such "babes" in the Kingdom of God). In the meantime, let us undertake this life-changing journey.

Section I

PEACE THROUGH RELATIONSHIP

The consideration of the possibility of knowing God personally is, at first glance, somewhat overwhelming. But when we read the Bible with this possibility in mind, it becomes apparent that this is what has been on God's heart from the very beginning. We are created for fellowship with Him, which is just another way of saying that he wants us to know him personally as He knows us personally. We are created to live with God in a personal loving relationship in an atmosphere of personal peace. Without personal peace we cannot continue in the loving relationship with our Lord that began when we received Him as our personal Savior. Shortly before His crucifixion, Jesus said to His disciples: "Peace I leave with you, my peace I give to you" (John 14:27). Then in the 15th chapter of John He gave that wonderful physical illustration of what our relationship with Him should be - He is the vine, we are to abide (unite) with Him as a branch unites with the vine. But we will not be able to continue in this abiding relationship without His gift of personal peace because personal peace clears away the confusion and frustration that Satan continually brings into our lives. Personal peace and knowing God personally go together. We cannot have one without the other.

Some of us have a measure of peace but most of us need more of it in our lives. There are many directions our paths can take in this life but for a Christian there should be only one - the path that leads to personal peace. It is the place of knowing God personally and it is the place that we can receive the abundance of His grace. Let us then, in this first section, begin with the journey to personal peace.

The Path to Personal Peace

1
Pathways of Life

In this life, each of us tread many pathways - some lead toward personal peace and others lead away from it - some lead to other pathways and some lead to a dead end. As we tread these pathways, personal peace can become distant and remote and difficult to find, but there is a path that leads straight toward that peace that "passes all understanding". It would be so easy if we could find this path early in life, but most of us walk many other paths before we reach that path that leads to personal peace.

It is my hope that, as we talk about these pathways of life, you will see life in a way you have never seen it before. By looking at the paths that lead to the path of personal peace, we shall see reality itself as we delve into the truths that God has revealed to us in the Bible. No matter where we are in life, regardless of how good or how bad the circumstances of our lives are, God has provided the signposts that will guide our paths to the path of personal relationship with Himself - the path that leads to peace. Let us then preview these pathways of life and see how they interconnect and lead to the path of personal peace.

All of us at some point in life, must walk the path that leads to self-identity. We simply must see that God really does love us and that

His love makes us somebody. Most of us
identify with things like traditions instead of
identifying with God's love. But, with a loving
relationship with our heavenly Father, we can
be secure in who we are and in our reason for
being.

Have you ever wondered about your
reason for being? If you have never asked the
question: Why was I born? I hope you will ask
it now. This is sort of a connecting path that
adds perspective to life. In becoming aware of
the meaning of life we see new purpose for
living - purpose that will help us avoid dead
ends and enable us to go on to be ourselves.

If we are to be free to be ourselves, it is
vital that we avoid the dead end that we
politely call resentment. To some degree, it
affects the lives of us all, and it tears down
meaningful relationships with men and with
God. The willingness to forgive is the pathway
that leads to right thinking and victory in the
Christian life.

Right thinking is the path that leads right
through a battlefield. The battle, of course, is
in the mind. You may not be aware of it, but
there is a constant struggle over what kind of
thoughts occupy our minds. Unless we
discipline our minds, it is not possible to
receive the strength God gives to overcome
fear and all the wrong emotions that are
caused by it.

Fear is so prevalent in our society that all of
us are affected by it in some way. We need to
tread the path that leads from fear to faith and
then go on to courage which is so necessary to
be successful in life. As we shall see, this will

take us directly to the path of personal peace. However, on the way, we shall see suffering all around us and become aware of the necessity to deal with it.

No one likes to suffer, but God allows it to enter our lives because it can actually work for our good. We must not leave the pathway by responding to the circumstances of suffering - we must see that suffering can work for our good if we respond to God. Responding to God requires the same kind of communication that is necessary with any other person. We must not only speak to Him, but we must hear Him. We need to walk the pathway that takes us close enough to God to hear His "still small voice" and to communicate with Him all through the day. If we are hearing God, we are able to receive His love and really become a loving person ourselves.

Jesus said that the most important thing we can do is to love God and that the second most important thing is to love our neighbor as we love ourselves (Matthew 22:37). If we are willing to do this, we come into full relationship with God and man - that means, we are walking the path that leads directly to personal peace.

Let us then examine this path of personal peace from the perspective of various paths that we have seen. Better still, let us do more than just examine - let us begin a journey across the pathways of life right into a better relationship with our heavenly Father.

2
Journey to Self-Identity

As we begin this journey across the pathways of life, we must of course, begin right where we are. Some know more about how they fit into life than others, but all of us, at one time or another, need to walk the path that leads to self-identity.

To participate in any kind of personal relationship, we should know who we are. Without knowing that, we cannot give of ourselves or relate to another person. Brothers and sisters are related because their blood ties them together, but they never become personally related until they give of themselves as a person - there must be a positive giving and receiving of each other. We can never be positive about giving of ourselves in any personal relationship unless we have positively identified ourselves.

Many people draw back from the reality of knowing who they are because our society teaches us that we are to conform to certain images of ourselves. Over time, people have come together in their self-images to participate in activities that have become traditional in our society - we call them traditions.

Many people, seeking to provide stability in their lives, hold on to traditions. In the stage play, *Fiddler on the Roof*, the father of a traditional Jewish family says: "Because of our traditions, everyone knows who he is and what God expects him to do." Well, that did not prove to be true in the stage play, and it is not true in real life. All of us are tempted to shape our attitudes and activities according to established practices instead of seeking God and His ways. Some traditions add a certain flavor to life but many people are guided by traditional standards instead of a personal relationship with a loving God. It is through God's love that we have identity. Tradition, much of the time, hides our need to know who we are and what God wants us to do.

If you are old enough to remember the decade of the 60's, you will know that young people were no longer accepting the traditions of family and "the establishment" - traditions that centered around such things as church, sports, cars, and homes. They could see, for instance, that it is hypocritical to keep a tradition of being "church-going people" without a real commitment to Jesus Christ. They didn't have many answers, but those young people did not let traditions confuse them; they looked at life and asked the question, "Who am I?"

Well, who are we? Do we have an identity? The answer is a resounding YES! It is God's love that makes us somebody. We are loved by the very one that created the world and placed us in it. It is God's love that identifies us with Him. He loves us as individuals - as persons. We are persons in the same way that God is a person because we have been created in God's likeness. "Then God said: Let us make man in our image, after our likeness" (Genesis 1:26 RSV). Not only that, in 1st John 4:16 (LB), we are told: "God is love, and anyone who lives in love is living with God and God is living in him." We are not only made in the likeness of God, but we can live with Him in a loving relationship. Christians can know who they are because they identify with God Himself through a personal relationship.

The problem of getting to know God personally is that we are not born with His kind of life. We know from the Bible that the life of God is spiritual life and that men everywhere are dead spiritually because they are separated from God by sin. Romans 3:23 KJV says, "all have sinned," and in Romans 6:23 KJV we read, "the wages of sin is death" - the result of sin is spiritual death! But the last part of this verse brings us face to face with the very life of God. It says, "the gift of God is eternal (spiritual) life through Jesus Christ our Lord." Because Christians have received this gift of spiritual life, they have a personal relationship with God - a Father-child relationship. But, just like a child with its earthly father, we need to learn to love our heavenly Father and accept His will for our lives. When a child really accepts a father's love, it wants to please him - to return that love and obey him. It is the same with our heavenly Father. Through loving obedience, the relationship is established, and we know for sure that we belong to God. It is from this sense of belonging that we know who we are.

It is not possible to know God and not know who we are. Christians have an identity that does not depend on the ways of man such as custom or tradition. They have peace and joy that comes out of the sure knowledge that God is their heavenly Father and that they are going to live with Him forever. If you are not certain about your identity, ask yourself if you ever really repented of your sin. Repentance, which is turning from the ways of man to the ways of God, opens the way to a personal relationship with Him (the path of peace).

If a child loves its parents, it is continually, year by year, turning from its own ways to the ways of its parents. In this process of repentance, a personal relationship develops. If this relationship does not develop, love between parent and child does not survive. It is no different with a child of God. Repentance is not something a Christian does just once - if it is real, it becomes a way of life and causes us to develop in our relationship to our heavenly Father. It is so easy to say, "Well I have done that." But before you say that, I urge you to search your heart and know that you are continually turning from your own ways to the ways of God. You may have made a profession of faith and maybe went on to be baptized. But if you do not have peace and joy and that sense of satisfaction and belonging that comes out of a developing relationship with God, you have a need to turn from your ways to His ways. Repentance is the only way to Jesus and Jesus is the only way to eternal life. He said, "I am the way, and the truth, and the life; no one comes to the Father, but by me. If you had known me, you would have known my Father also" (John 14:6,7 RSV). My prayer is that you will make sure that you know Jesus - that you are a child of God. Tell Him that you are sinful and that you want to spend the rest of your days turning from your ways to His ways. Realize that because Jesus paid the penalty for your sin on the cross, the result of your sin doesn't have to be spiritual death. Open your heart and receive His gift of eternal life. Then, with a thankful heart, begin to return His love. When you seek to please Him, by committing yourself to Him in loving obedience, you will realize that the relationship has been established and that you belong to God and His family. Because of this belonging, you will never need to ask the question: Who am I?

In knowing who we are, we can begin to see reality in life. Out of this self-identity, it is now possible to see much more meaning and purpose in life - to see that God has a plan for our lives and earnestly desires to prepare us to live with Him forever.

3
Pausing to Observe the Meaning of Life

As we tread our way across these various pathways, I believe it is good to pause and observe this wonder that we call life. Over the years, I have asked many people, "Have you ever wondered why we are on this earth?" Some had never thought about it, but most had pondered the question and were interested in looking closer at the meaning of life. From the Bible, we know the rebellious history of man and God's loving purpose for His Creation. The problem is that we, the created, tend to ignore God and go our own way. But when man decides to open himself to his Creator, the very meaning of life is opened to him. Only then can we see how destitute we are without God and how much we need a personal relationship with Him.

In the beginning, Adam and Eve had a personal relationship with God - they understood when He said, "of the tree of the knowledge of good and evil you shall not eat, for in the day you eat of it you shall die" (Genesis 2:17 RSV). Only God knows what is good or bad for our lives. But in their disobedience, Adam and Eve believed Satan's lie. In Genesis 3:4,5 (RSV), Satan said, "You will not die. For God knows that when you eat of it (the tree of the knowledge of good and evil) your eyes will be opened, and you will be like God, knowing good and evil." Their desire was to be like God - to be equal to God - to be their own god.

Well, they ate of that tree, and man has had trouble and pain ever since. Even though Adam and Eve lived many years physically, they lost their spiritual life that day. They separated themselves from their Creator by believing that they knew what was good or bad, and so they refused to obey God. That is what the Bible calls sin. It says: "as sin came into the world through one man and death through sin, and so death spread to all men because all men sinned" (Romans 5:12 RSV). This sin that brings spiritual death has affected every human being since the beginning - "all have sinned and come short of the glory of God" (Romans 3:23 KJV). If we live with sin and without spiritual life, there can be no personal relationship with God. Without that relationship, we are all adrift in the sea of life without anyone to really depend on. To continue without that relationship, is to get by the best way we can until life is over - never knowing the true meaning of life or the plan God has for our lives.

Of course, God knew very well men would go their own way and try to be their own god. So He began working with them right where they were - teaching each generation a little more about his plan for mankind. As more people came into relationship with Him, God began to reveal that He intended to pay the penalty for man's sin Himself. That penalty was death, so He was to come to earth, as a human being, to die for the sin of the world. As the Bible account progresses, prophets spelled out the details of the coming "Messiah." In the 53rd chapter of Isaiah, we are given a detailed prophecy about the coming of the Messiah and His death. Later, we read the account of how He came and willingly died on a Roman cross for your sin and mine. Then, exactly according to prophecy, He was resurrected by the power of God. His name, of course is Jesus Christ.

Because Jesus paid the death penalty and lives again, God offers eternal life to those who repent or turn away from sin. Eternal life is a free gift of God to those who don't want to go their own way anymore - to those who believe that Jesus' death paid for their sin and who receive Him into their hearts and lives. "The wages of sin is death; but the gift of God is eternal life through Jesus Christ our Lord" (Romans 6:23 KJV).

What, then, are we seeing as we follow the biblical account of God's great plan for man? Why is He so concerned about this life He has given us, and what is the meaning of it? Some say we are here to eat, drink, and be merry and then just die. But God says we are here to be part of this glorious plan that He has for our lives. The Scripture says: "Therefore if any man be in Christ, he is a new creature: old things are passed away; behold, all things are become new" (2 Corinthians 5:17 KJV). A Christian has a new kind of life - the very life of God which is spiritual life. We are on this earth to be "born again" of the Spirit of God. Then we are to grow and mature in that spiritual life because we have a personal relationship with God. The God of the universe is a Person who loves us personally and desires our fellowship. Through that relationship, He makes it possible to grow and become all we are created to be. Through that relationship, He wants to use this time that we have on earth to prepare us to live with Him forever. That makes life so meaningful that all of us should be concerned about the time we spend outside of that personal relationship.

It is evident that the most important thing we can do in this life is to develop our relationship with God. God's standard for any relationship is "agape" love. "Agape" love always seeks the very best for the other person - it is centered on what is good for them instead of what is good for the self. Self-centered relationships are always warped and seldom touch reality. It is not possible to be ourselves if our love is centered on ourselves - but more than that, a self-centered person has nothing in common with our heavenly Father.

Probably the most damaging and most prevalent form of self-centeredness is resentment. As we shall see, anyone who holds resentment against another, holds himself in bondage. We must be free to be ourselves if we are to walk the path to personal peace.

4
The Pathway to Freedom

Personal peace always dwells in an atmosphere of freedom - freedom to be ourselves. Most of us, to some degree, need this freedom. The problem is that the pathway that leads there is sometimes blocked - not by others but by our own doing. Almost all of us, from time to time, allow ourselves to be caught up in some form of resentment. If we hold resentment against others, we are not free to be ourselves with them. Resentment not only blocks our freedom to be ourselves, but it blocks out meaningful relationships - it is like a wall between men and between men and God.

Because resentment is so destructive in people's lives, it has been called a "cancer of the soul." It not only limits our personal peace, but it becomes a temptation to those around us because the natural response to resentment is resentment. If others resent us, we feel rejected - and that makes us want to resent and reject them.

Some of us have been rejected (or thought we have) since early childhood. All of us experience rejection from time to time. This causes anger and all kinds of negative emotions. We then say things and do things that we would never say or do if we did not have this cancer in our soul. It is so easy to resent what others say or do and just reject them. We feel we have some kind of right to resent those around us simply because we have been resented and rejected by someone who, probably, had previously been hurt himself. The hurt always begins in the emotions, but there are also mental, physical, and spiritual consequences.

Failure to forgive people who have hurt us brings on all those negative emotions - the result is anxiety and depression. If this goes on, the turmoil in the mind prevents the recognition of our need to forgive. Ultimately, failure to forgive brings us into mental bondage because those we resent so occupy our minds that they are actually controlling our thoughts. In addition, all of this can disrupt the chemical balance in our bodies and cause all kinds of physical suffering. But the most disastrous consequence is a rupture in our relationship with God because resentment is hate and hate makes us unable to love our heavenly Father. The Bible says: "If a man say, I love God, and hateth his brother, he is a liar: for he that loveth not his brother whom he hath seen, how can he love God whom he hath not seen.?" (I John 4:20 KJV). The only relationship that is possible with God is a loving relationship. If we fail to forgive, the hate in our hearts and minds cuts us off from God because we have no personal relationship with Him. The irony is that when we are resentful, we only hurt ourselves. We always reap what we sow.

There is a spiritual law as binding as the law of gravity. It is the law of sowing and reaping: "Whatsoever a man soweth, that shall he reap" (Galatians 6:7 KJV). Jesus said, "if you forgive people their trespasses - that is, their reckless and willful sins, leaving them, letting them go and giving up resentment - your heavenly Father will also forgive you" (Matthew 6:14 Amplified Bible). We cannot reap forgiveness until we sow it. In all of life we reap what we sow. If we resent and reject, that is what we reap. If we forgive, we are forgiven by both God and man - then a loving relationship takes place. If we are to walk the path that leads to peace, we must decide to forgive.

Forgiveness is wiping the slate clean and transferring the responsibility for any punishment to God - it is a definite, conscious act of the will - a decision. But it must begin in the heart - we must want to forgive, or else it does not happen.

Many times in my life, I have convinced myself that I had forgiven only to find that I still had that "telltale," critical attitude. I had forgiven in my head but not in my heart. If we are critical or prone to notice the faults of others, our forgiveness is counterfeit, because we do not want to forgive in our heart. We must see the plight of people who hurt us and actually get on their side.

Think for a minute how people think. In their minds, most people tend to justify everything they say and do. They rationalize their behavior even when others are hurt - sometimes they become very sophisticated in the way they convince themselves that what they say and do is justified. Sometimes they are not even aware of having hurt someone else because they are caught in this web of unreal thinking. When they reach this point, they have become insensitive to others - then they become unresponsive to both God and man. Some people wreck their entire lives as they persist in this unreal behavior. If we see that they are victims of this kind of thinking (that all of us are guilty of from time to time), any hurt we may receive from them will be less offensive to us - we can actually identify with them. Then, with love and mercy, our hearts will begin to soften, and we will actually want to forgive. We can know we have forgiven others when we see their plight and, in mercy, have compassion for them. Jesus said, in His sermon on the mount, "Blessed are the merciful, for they shall receive mercy" (Matthew 5:7 NAS).

Another thing that helps us to forgive is the realization that most people's offenses toward us are a direct result of their own resentment. Because they have been hurt previously, they develop a critical attitude that causes them to reject others. Out of that rejection, they say things and do things that hurt us and cause our resentment toward them. It is a vicious cycle - more than that, it is a disease that is loose in the world, and, when it infects us, it spreads like cancer in the bloodstream. Also like cancer, it takes many forms and may be difficult to recognize.

David said in Psalm 139:23 (KJV), "Search me, O God, and know my heart." We are not very good at searching and knowing our hearts, but God is, and if we ask Him to show us our resentment and unforgiveness, He will. If we confess these sins and ask forgiveness, God will forgive us and "cleanse us from all unrighteousness" (1 John 1:9 KJV). But that is not enough. We have to stop sinning. We cannot stay on this path to freedom unless we stop the critical attitude that is unforgiveness. We cannot be free to be ourselves until our heart attitude says, "I forgive you."

If we react to others with understanding, mercy, and forgiveness, the power and love of God enters in and attitudes change. Then the situation changes and Godly character prevails.

The Bible says, "Be ye kind one to another, tenderhearted, forgiving one another, even as God for Christ's sake hath forgiven you" (Ephesians 4:32 KJV). Forgiveness is something that is required of us by a loving God who knows that we cannot be the person He created us to be unless we are willing and even eager to forgive. We must have a forgiving attitude and a desire to love people by forgiving them. Giving and receiving forgiveness is the key that sets us free to fellowship with God and to walk that path that leads to peace. But that is not possible if we do not guard our thinking.

We must be constantly aware that there is a battle in our minds over whether we forgive or not. Even as we choose to forgive, we must be sure to stay on the path as we pass through the battle over the thoughts that we allow in our minds.

5
Passing Through the Battle

Have you ever thought of your mind as a battleground? Well it is! There is a constant struggle of the will over what kind of thoughts we will allow in our minds. As we follow this pathway through the battleground of our minds, we will see very clearly the importance of our freedom to make choices and how this freedom determines the outcome of our lives.

By giving us a "free will," God has made us responsible for the kind of thinking that goes on in our minds. We must decide between selfish thoughts or Godly thoughts. If we do not deliberately choose Godly thoughts, our minds become preoccupied with ourselves and the faults of others. The Bible says, "as a man thinketh in his heart so is he." What we are, our very character, is determined by what we think in our heart, and what we think in our heart is determined by the choices we make.

Our thinking is like an unbroken horse that is useless until it comes under the discipline of the bridle. Without the bridle of discipline, our thinking becomes as upsetting as the unbroken horse; then wrong emotions play havoc in our lives. The result is fear, anger, resentment, criticism, judgment, self-pity, depression, and all the wrong decisions and wrong actions that go with them. We must fight the battle for discipline in our minds.

You may say: that's like a war in my mind, and you would be right. But war is not so bad when you are victorious. What is bad is the defeat we experience when we refuse the resources God has made available to us. The war is no less real - the difference is: you are defeated and don't know it. That's tragic when we realize that victory in the mind can be ours in the power of God's Holy Spirit.

The problem is that most people think that the power of God's Holy Spirit is a kind of magic that comes in and fixes things. That is not true! God insists that we do our part in this battle in the mind. Our minds are not some kind of captive computers nor are we robots. Christians are part of the family of God, and our heavenly Father will not violate our will. He has made us free to choose, and even free to decide not to choose. Because of their indifference, many Christians decide not to choose in many situations. They do not realize that God wants us to use our freedom to choose - to cooperate with Him in the battle for right thinking. It is true that we cannot discipline our minds in right thinking without the power of God's Holy Spirit, but God doesn't enter in until we decide to do our part. We must participate in this battle to be renewed in our minds.

As Christians, we are not to copy the thinking of the world, but we are to be new and different with a fresh newness in our thoughts. The Scripture puts it this way: "Do not be conformed to this world but be transformed by the renewal of your mind" (Romans 12:2a RSV). Again, in Ephesians 4:23 (KJV), it says, "Be renewed in the spirit of your mind." We can be renewed by bringing discipline to our minds, knowing that we will be transformed in the process. If we stop conforming our thinking and thus ourselves to this world and to the selfish ways and customs of society, and ask God for the power to conform to His ways, we will surely be transformed. Society says, "don't be different" - God says, "be transformed."

Transformation, to many, sounds supernatural and beyond their reach, so they don't reach for it at all - they refuse the resources of God. We all need to see the reality of the Christian life - it is supernatural. The Christian lives with, and is empowered by, God Who is supernatural. If we do our part which is natural, He will do His part which is supernatural. The question then is: What is our part in this renewal and transformation?

In Ephesians 4:22 through 24, there are three steps we can take to be transformed in our thinking. However these steps can only be taken by those who have truly submitted their lives to the lordship of Jesus Christ. The power of the Holy Spirit is not available to those who will not let God control their lives. Having said that, let us go on to examine these steps.

First of all, our part is to put aside our old way of thinking which is self-centered and deceitful - we deceive ourselves sometimes by believing our motives are for the benefit of others when they are for our own benefit. Second, our attitude, which controls our thinking, must constantly change for the better - we must become more and more interested in the welfare of others and want the very best for them. Third, we must take on the new nature that was made available to us when we were "born again". This, of course, involves actions as well as thoughts, but we must begin by thinking the way God would have us to think. We must, more and more, refuse to think thoughts that are inconsistent with the Christian life. If we put aside our old way of thinking, develop a loving attitude, and put on God's way of thinking, God will surely do His part in our transformation from wrong thinking to right thinking.

By now you are probably saying, "I cannot do those three things," and you would be right. None of us can overcome our self-centered thought patterns alone - it takes the supernatural power of God's Holy Spirit to make that a reality. But if we step out in faith to take these three steps, we can ask for, and receive, the fullness of the Holy Spirit. The Scripture says: "you shall receive power when the Holy Spirit has come upon you" (Acts 1:8a RSV). The very power of God will make us able to progressively accomplish the transformation of our thinking which will bring us into a close personal relationship with our heavenly Father. By thinking the way He thinks, we can have real fellowship with Him. This is the path that leads to peace, and, if we stay on it, our entire lives will be transformed.

Having begun this process of transformation, new possibilities are opened in the way we think and live. An example of this is found in Paul's admonition to the Philippians. He said, "Don't worry about anything; tell God your needs and don't forget to thank Him for His answers. If you do this you will experience God's peace, which is far more wonderful than the human mind can understand. His peace will keep your thoughts and your hearts quiet and at rest as you trust in Christ Jesus" (Philippians 4:6,7 LB). Then, in the very next verse, he tells us the way God wants us to think. Here in one verse is a way to apply the bridle of discipline to our minds: "whatever is true, whatever is honorable, whatever is just, whatever is pure, whatever is lovely, whatever is gracious, if there is any excellence, if there is anything worthy of praise, think about these things" (Philippians 4:8 RSV). This can be a check list as we step out in the power of the Holy Spirit to apply the bridle of discipline to our minds - but it will take persistence and courage.

All of us, to one degree or another, have a need for more courage in order to participate in this battle in the mind. Fear is very prevalent in our society - it affects our thoughts and our actions more than most of us realize - it also saps most of us of the courage we need even to enter the battle. If we are to have victory in the mind, most of us must first tread that path that leads from fear to courage.

6
The Path from Fear to Courage

E.Stanley Jones, in his book *The Way*, says, " Fear harnessed to constructive ends may be constructive. When we use fear and control it, then it is good. When fear uses us and controls us, then it is bad. Fear has three things against it: (1) It is disease-producing. (2) It is paralyzing to effort. (3) It is useless." The thing God meant for good becomes distorted in our lives, producing disease and sometimes paralyzing our efforts. As fear becomes part of our thinking, it manifests itself in ways that sometimes we fail to recognize. If you think about it, I believe that you will agree with me that worry is fear - fear of the future, fear of failure, fear of people, fear of ill-health, and so on. Fear will be added to fear as long as we allow that kind of thinking in our minds. Fear has a way of making itself comfortable in our lives and multiplying itself. We often live with it over such an extended period of time that it seems natural, and we allow it to affect everything we say and do. As long as we are exercising fear, we cannot exercise faith, and, without faith, we withdraw and lose the victory. It is absolutely vital in the Christian life to harness fear to constructive ends - to replace distorted fear with faith, and to walk the path that leads from fear to courage.

One of the best examples of courage that I know of is that of a young man in the Bible. This young man was not yet out of his teens the day he faced a giant of a man in mortal combat. The young man of course was David. Samuel had anointed him to become king of Israel, and, out of that experience, the Bible says, David received the fullness and power of God's Holy Spirit (I Samuel 16:13). He stood there, fearless before Goliath, knowing that, in the Lord, he had the victory.

In my life, I have lost the victory many times because fear dominated my thinking. In looking back, I see that I often withdrew from the contest simply because I lacked God's power to overcome fear. Because fear can become part of our thinking, it is very easy to overlook the fact that a close personal relationship with God will cast out fear and give us the courage to be bold as lions.

David's testimony to Saul in the 17th chapter of 1st Samuel (RSV) was that he had fought lions and bears that attacked his sheep. In verse 37, he said: "The Lord who delivered me from the paw of the lion and from the paw of the bear, will deliver me from the hand of this Philistine." I believe we can see a progression here. David must have begun with fear that seems natural to all of us, but he didn't stop there; he went on to exercise the faith God had given him. Out of his faith that the Lord would deliver him, courage emerged, and he became bold as a lion. The progression, then, is fear to faith and from faith to courage. When fear is gone, we are free to exercise faith. When faith is exercised, the power of God's Holy Spirit enters in, and we become courageous. I believe that it was no less than the power of God that enabled David to say to Goliath, "You come to me with a sword and a spear, but I come to you in the name of the LORD of the armies of heaven and of Israel - the very God whom you have defied" (I Samuel 17:45 LB). There was no fear in that statement - if there had been, there would have been no courage. We need to handle our fear, then, in a way that makes it possible to exercise the faith that God gives to all of His children. The Scripture, I believe, is very clear about how we are to handle fear in our lives. It recognizes fear as a good thing in its proper place, but fear is also recognized as a bad thing when it is distorted and begins to control us. Fear was very much on the mind of Jesus during His earthly ministry. This is apparent in the Scripture as we hear Him use such phrases as "fear not" or "peace be unto you" or "have faith in God." Our Lord was very sensitive to the way we distort things in our lives. If we are to please Him, we must be rid of the distortion of fear.

We have already seen that there is a progression from fear to faith and from faith to courage. But how do we get rid of fear in order to make a beginning? The Bible says, in 1 John 4:18 (KJV), that "There is no fear in love; but perfect love casteth out fear." Perfect love is God's love completed in His children. We must realize that God really does love us individually. Knowing this, we can begin to receive His love. However, the love we receive is not perfected until we begin to return God's love. That is when love is completed or made perfect. The completion of that love becomes a personal relationship with God, because love is being given and received. There is the key. If we develop a personal relationship with God, fear is cast out, our faith emerges, and courage comes alive.

David and all the great men of the Bible were great because of their faith and courage - faith and courage that was a result of knowing God personally. That is, they received God's love as individuals, and as individuals, gave God their love. Out of this relationship, their fears dropped away, and courage made it possible for them to be greatly used by God. They did more than just recognize a truth about God's love - they did something about it by giving God their love. God's love was perfected or completed in them, and this gave them the courage to become what God wanted them to be.

The Bible says that God has a plan for our lives. It also says that "old things pass away," that "all things become new," and that we are to become "new creatures in Christ Jesus." All through the Bible, we are told, over and over again, that the Christian life is to be radically different than life was before we became a Christian. The response of the individual Christian to this theme of the Bible varies according to each personality, but there is a response that is absolutely necessary if we are to become what God wants us to be. That response is courage. We need courage to stand fast in our faith not only in the world but among Christians that do not stand fast in their faith. Millions of God's children have begun their Christian lives with hope and joy only to find, at some point, that fear neutralized their faith and their courage. We need courage to live our lives before God instead of living them before friends, neighbors, and family. Courage just is not present in our lives unless love is being perfected or completed in us.

The very first thing God wants us to be is a loving people. The Pharisees asked Jesus what the greatest commandment was. "Jesus replied, ' Love the Lord your God with all your heart, soul, and mind.' This is the first and greatest commandment. The second most important is similar: 'Love your neighbor as much as you love yourself.' All the other commandments and all the demands of the prophets stem from these two laws and are fulfilled if you obey them. Keep only these and you will find that you are obeying all the others" (Matthew 22:37-40 LB). There, in a nutshell, is what God wants us to become. Love is woven through the whole creation because God is love. Love is the very fabric of the Christian life. We can talk about it and explain it, as I am doing now, but if our love is not completed, we will never have the courage to go on in the Christian life. Our churches are filled with folks who have never had the courage to become what God wants them to be. I was just such a person for many years until one day I realized that I did not love God. I had accepted His gift of eternal life, but I never received His love much less love Him in return. I simply did not have that personal relationship that comes out of a love that has been made complete. As a result, courage was lacking in my life. I was so filled with fear that I could hardly share my knowledge of Jesus Christ with others. Finally, I realized that God really does love me - that, in the power of His Holy Spirit, I could begin to fulfill the command to love God and to love my neighbor as myself. As we open ourselves to the Holy Spirit, we are able to return the love that we receive from God. Then fear is cast out, and faith and courage come forth.

I see now that courage is available to every child of God. The God of David is our God, and our God makes all of His blessings available to all of His children. We can have the same courage David had. Like David, we can stand fearless before every obstacle knowing that, in the Lord, we have the victory. Like David, we can be... bold as lions.

Boldness to some people seems brash and is not a desirable quality, but that is not what the Bible teaches. It says: "The wicked flee when no one is pursuing, but the righteous are bold as a lion" (Proverbs 28:1 NAS). The person that is living in God's will has a boldness that enables him to stay on the path even in the midst of suffering. The bold Christian can pass right through the suffering in life to the blessings of God.

7
Going Through Suffering to Blessing

Without suffering, most of us are not very responsive to God. There have been times in my life that I ignored God because things seemed to be the way I wanted them to be. I was not aware that my heavenly Father tends to bless His children much like a physical father; He supplies certain needs whether we respond to Him or not, but many of His blessings come only as we seek Him in a childlike way. Without suffering, most of us would never learn to seek God at all - so, the path to blessing sometimes passes right through suffering.

All of us experience a certain amount of suffering - we not only suffer from accidents and disease, but we also suffer emotional pain which we generally refer to as anxiety or tension. No one likes to suffer, but suffering can actually work for our good if we respond to God. If it doesn't work for our good, then of course, we suffer for nothing. Many times I have suffered from tension and anxiety which eventually caused pain and suffering in my physical body - I didn't respond to God - I responded to the circumstances. The result was not spiritual growth - it was physical and emotional pain.

Suffering or pain is a warning. Whether it be a burned finger on a hot stove or an emotional pain that explodes in a resentful attack on our neighbor, pain is a sign that something is wrong. Little children take their hurt feelings or burned fingers to their parents - that is exactly what our heavenly Father wants His children to do with their suffering. The little child can receive comfort for his burned finger and instruction about hot stoves from its earthly parents; in the same way, God's children can be comforted and instructed in the midst of the trials and tribulations that all of us face in life.

But there is more than comfort and instruction available to Christians. God desires to bless us "beyond what we can ask or think." But we need to obey Him to receive His blessings. Listen to what the Bible says: "Behold, I set before you this day a blessing and a curse: the blessing, if you obey the commandments of the Lord your God, which I command you this day, and the curse, if you do not obey the commandments of the Lord your God, but turn aside from the way which I command you this day" (Deuteronomy 11:26-28 RSV). If we turn aside from the way God wants us to go, we not only rebel against Him personally, but we rebel against the physical and spiritual laws that govern His creation. If we are going to receive God's blessings, we must choose to obey Him and be in harmony with His creation. He has a plan for all of our lives, but it is in accordance with His laws. When we are obedient and fulfill this plan, our lives are filled with God's blessings. Out of obedience, we can expect health, prosperity, and harmony with God and man. Out of disobedience, we can expect disease, accidents, divorce, worry, rejection, and all manner of human suffering. Almost from the very beginning of man's life on earth, man has been inclined to disobey God and go his own way. The result is all the suffering and pain and hurt that we see around us. Out of our freedom to choose, we simply must choose to love and obey God.

Like a little child, we need to be willing to obey and even want to obey. Little children are not always obedient, but, if they love their parents, they will have a deep-down desire to obey them. We need this desire to obey our heavenly Father - but to be real, it must come from love. Jesus said in John 14:15 (RSV), "If you love me, you will keep my commandments." He also said, in the very next verse, that this loving obedience would result in the Holy Spirit coming into our lives. To love and obey God is to be in harmony with Him and His plans for our lives - then by His Spirit, He will cause things to work together for our good. In Romans 8:28 (KJV), the Bible puts it like this: "All things work together for good to them that love God, to them who are the called according to His purpose" (loving obedience). Not only some things but all things - even suffering - become beneficial to us as long as we love God and seek to obey Him.

In the midst of suffering, it is easy to forget about loving and obeying God - the natural thing to do is to dash around trying to find our own solution. But the rewards of this loving obedience are great; not only will all things work together for our good, but we will grow spiritually in the process. We all know that the physical stress of lifting weight causes our muscles to grow; in the same way, the stress of suffering can cause us to grow spiritually if we respond to God. In response, God will set our feet on that path that leads to peace - a close personal relationship with Himself. This close relationship is, in itself, spiritual growth because it produces much spiritual fruit in our lives.

Spiritual growth is indeed a great blessing, but there is more. We grow emotionally and have better physical health because our emotional and physical natures are subject to our spiritual nature. As we draw closer and closer to God, we produce more and more spiritual fruit. If we take only the first three fruits listed in Galatians 5:22, we can see a great effect upon our emotional life. If we truly produce love, joy, and peace, this spiritual fruit will eliminate emotional instability which is primarily responsible for the chemical imbalance that causes so much physical suffering.

In every circumstance of life, there are emotional, physical, and spiritual blessings. When suffering comes, it is either working for our good, or we are suffering for nothing. Is there suffering in your life now? Are you reacting to the circumstances of your suffering, or are you reacting to the love of God? The Bible says that we can love God because He loves us first. We must ask God to teach us to return His love just like little children learn to return the love of their parents. We can learn to love by example, and God is the best example in the whole universe. When we really experience God's love, it is easy to love

Him in return. If we do this, we will never fall off of the path, as we go through suffering, to the blessings of God.

As we experience more and more of God's blessings, it becomes evident that the loving relationship that we have with Him is the only consistent way to receive from Him. There is not only communication in prayer and Bible reading that was never there before, but we can know the mind of God concerning the issues of our lives. As we walk this path to peace, it is vital that we maintain fellowship with the one who wants to bless us so abundantly.

8
Fellowship on the Path

I think that it goes without saying that all Christians have some kind of relationship with God - we are all standing on the path that leads to personal peace. But just being on the path does not always mean we will reach our destination - any personal relationship that goes anywhere is a two-way communication that becomes fellowship. The kind of relationship that leads to the peace of God is more than just speaking to Him - many people do that; if we are to have fellowship with Him, we must also hear Him.

All of us have a great need to hear that "still small voice" of God so that we can receive His guidance and know more and more about the plan He has for our lives. We need communication with Him all through the day - allowing Him to speak to us by placing His thoughts in our minds. But more than that, we need to live in His peace as we fellowship with Him day by day and hour by hour.

If you think about it, I believe you will agree that fellowship takes place only when we make an effort to hear the other person - if we are going to be in fellowship with God, we must spend the time and effort that is necessary to walk close enough to hear His voice. Jesus put it like this: "I have been standing at the door and I am constantly knocking. If anyone hears me calling him and opens the door, I will come in and fellowship with him" (Revelation 3:20 LB). It is plain, from the words of Jesus, that He seeks to fellowship with us, but He expects us to hear His voice and open the door. The problem is that our sophisticated ways are so foreign to the ways of God that it is difficult to hear Him or even know that the door is closed.

If we are to hear God, we must humble ourselves as a little child. We try so hard to be sophisticated adults, not realizing that God desires for us to be "as little children." He does not look upon His people as sophisticated adults - if we are Christians we are "children of God." Of course, older children can become rebellious, but little children, one or two years old, are naturally trusting, teachable, and submissive with their parents. All of us need to ask ourselves: Is that the way I am with my heavenly Father - or, am I a sophisticated adult? God wants His people to be responsible for what they say and do - but, He wants them to be as little children in their hearts. Jesus said: "Anyone who humbles himself as the little child, is the greatest in the Kingdom of Heaven" (Matthew 18:4 LB). The desire to be sophisticated adults makes it difficult to humble ourselves as a little child. But, the way to hear God is through an on-going, Father-child relationship. Our part is to hear the voice of Jesus and "open the door" with a trusting, teachable, and submissive attitude. Then, as Jesus enters in, the power of His Holy Spirit "helps us in our infirmities" and we are able to fellowship with our risen Lord. Then Jesus leads us into that Father-child relationship with our heavenly Father. Through Jesus and the power of the Holy Spirit, we can hear the voice of our heavenly Father and enter into our great privilege of fellowship with the God of the universe.

It is, of course, the in filling of the Holy Spirit that is needed by so many Christians that desire to hear God and to enter into this fellowship. When we receive Jesus, we receive salvation and the indwelling of the Holy Spirit, but the fullness of the Holy Spirit never becomes a reality until we make Jesus absolute Lord over our lives. It is then, and only then, that Jesus fills us full and overflowing with His Holy Spirit - the Bible says that He will literally...baptize us with His Holy Spirit (Acts 11:16). The fellowship that follows is truly a precious and wondrous thing - it is the path that leads directly to personal peace. Anxiety and emotional conflict leave - then satisfaction and thankfulness come forth from a sense of well-being that is beyond description. This peace is such a blessed thing that many who experience it think that it will, of itself, continue for all time. That would be true if it were not for our natural bent toward thinking and acting our way instead of God's way. Because we have this natural tendency to fall away from the fullness of the Holy Spirit, it is necessary to respond to the knocking of Jesus again and again - to open the door with a trusting, teachable, and submissive attitude. If we are vigilant, we can come back into fellowship as soon as we fall away, but, because God has made that our responsibility, it is up to us to do our part in maintaining this loving relationship. There is this one thing about it: once we begin to hear God and respond to His love, the closeness of the relationship makes it easier to stay in fellowship with Him.

Actually, it is easier to stay in close fellowship with God than it is in human relationships because God's love is constant. He keeps on loving us no matter what we say or do - it is our love that is always in doubt. We must be willing to do our part in this loving relationship if we are going to stay on the path that leads to peace.

9
Staying on the Path

The pathway to personal peace is sometimes rocky and hard to travel - for most of us, it is difficult to stay on the path. The essence of all personal relationships should be love, and that is where we have difficulty. We relate to family, friends, and to God in various ways, but if these personal relationships are not characterized by love, they do not survive. Many times we begin a relationship with love and then wander off the path as we drift back into our self-centered ways. If we are going to stay on the path to personal peace, we must be willing to continue in love in all of our relationships - especially our relationship with God.

To continue in a loving relationship is not easy, because we tend to center our thinking around our own wants and needs. Because of this, some people tend to look at love in a general sort of way. They give of themselves in the beginning - then withdraw; yet, in the midst of withdrawn love, they are firmly convinced that they have a loving relationship. Love is not a "once for all" thing - if it is real, it grows and matures in a give-and-take relationship. If there is not a giving and receiving of love, the relationship grows stale and dies. The wonderful thing about our relationship with God is that He never withdraws His love.

We can receive God's love at any time - He is always right there offering us the abundance of His loving nature. That means that we can be in relationship with Him anytime we choose. Some Christians have never entered into this loving relationship - others have entered in and withdrawn - but all of us, if we choose to do so, can enter in today and tomorrow - and all of the rest of the days of our lives.

Someone has said that love is something you do and that is true. Love is a conscious or subconscious decision to give of ourselves to another person. Some people give of themselves easily, because they have a desire to be a loving person; this desire causes them to continue in various relationships all through life because they have decided to love. Although our emotions are very much involved, love begins as an act of the will. As we have seen, this is illustrated in the Bible by an encounter that Jesus had with the Pharisees. They asked Him: which is the greatest of the Ten Commandments? His reply was: "Thou shalt love the Lord thy God with all thy heart, and with all thy soul, and with all thy mind" (Matthew 22:37 KJV). The most important thing we can do is to love God, but we must be willing, or we will never obey that commandment. If we are willing to love God, our lives can be transformed day by day. Why? Because, in being willing to love, we open ourselves to the possibility of receiving love, and love, especially the love of God, does more to change lives than anything in the whole world.

If we are to stay on the path to personal peace, we must see the reality of what God says to us over and over again in the Bible - that He really does love us personally. During His ministry here on the earth, Jesus' life was a continuing example of how God loves us personally. In reading through the Gospels, we can see that His relationship with people was sometimes characterized by "tough love" and sometimes by compassionate love, but He always had a selfless concern for them as individuals.

In the parable of the prodigal son (Luke 15:11-32), we are given a beautiful illustration of how our heavenly Father loves us personally. Of course there is other meaning in this parable, but it is a wonderful illustration of God's love as it is described in other parts of the Bible. The rebellious son, who had left home, was now returning to a forgiving father who desired only to give to him and celebrate with him. If you read the parable with this in mind, I think you will become more aware of the warm personal love that our heavenly Father has for each one of us.

It is important for every one of us to let the truth about God's love penetrate our tough exterior - to let Him love us personally. As we receive the wonderful blessing of God's love, we willingly love Him in return. With God's love as our personal possession and our love as His personal possession, we not only complete the relationship, but we can continue in it all the days of our lives. If we continue in it, we will surely stay on the path to peace.

Because the world around us is continually drawing us away from this loving relationship, it is important that we do our part to maintain it. The normal response to God's love is to praise Him - to recognize Him for who He is. David knew this and went on to become one of the great men of the Bible. He said in Psalm 34:1 (KJV), " I will bless the Lord at all times: His praise shall continually be in my mouth." He knew that praise was an integral part of his fellowship with God - it is no different with us.

Praising God, of course, varies with the individual personality - some people find that it is helpful to read David's Psalms - others hum or sing Scripture songs and hymns all through the day. An attitude of thankfulness will keep all of us continually aware of the great benefit of God's love - praise and thanksgiving always go together when we truly respond to God's love.

We know that David had a close personal relationship with God over a long period of time. From the Scripture, it is evident that he maintained this relationship by responding to God's love with praise and thanksgiving. Because of this, depression and negative emotions ceased to be a part of his life. He stayed on the path, and personal peace was the result. Personal peace will also be the result in our lives if we stay on the path. Let us then take a close look at this peace and discover why it comes to those who are willing to maintain a continuous, loving relationship with our heavenly Father.

10
Living in Peace

Most of us, from time to time, experience some sort of peace, but that is not enough to live a successful Christian life. We need that deep-down contentment that makes us satisfied with who we are and what we have. We need to experience more and more personal peace - we need to learn to live in the peace that "passes all understanding." Since this peace looms before us on the pathway, let us look at it in a way that we can discover more about what it is, where it comes from, and how our relationship with God can keep us in perfect peace.

Billy Graham once told a story about a raging storm. He said: "The sea was beating against the rocks in huge, dashing waves. The lightning was flashing, the thunder was roaring, and the wind was blowing; but the little bird was sound asleep in the crevice of the rock- its head tucked serenely under its wing. "That," he said, "is peace - to be able to sleep in the storm." That is a beautiful picture in words - a graphic example of how a Christian can be an over comer through the storms of life. But let us look closer at our own peace in our own lives.

Personal peace is the peace of God - it is a state of well-being that is free from anxiety, emotional conflict, and struggles with the conscience. Personal peace dwells in the midst of uncomplicated lives and produces hope, love, and the "Joy of the Lord." But where does it come from? Jesus said: "My peace I give unto you: not as the world giveth, give I unto you. Let not your heart be troubled, neither let it be afraid" (John 14:27 KJV). Sometimes people settle for a form of peace, which is no more than a feeling of being accepted by other people, but real peace comes from God.

Many centuries ago, the prophet Isaiah made this astounding statement: "Thou wilt keep him in perfect peace, whose mind is stayed on thee" (Isaiah 26:3 KJV). If our minds are stayed on God - if we make Him and His ways the center of our thinking, He will keep us in perfect peace. Well, you may ask; How can I make God and His ways the center of my thinking? The answer is relationship - a continuous personal relationship with our heavenly Father.

As we have seen, all Christians that have not wandered away from God, that have an obedient attitude toward Him, have a personal relationship with Him - a Father-child relationship. This Father-child relationship takes place much like a young, earthly child with its father. It doesn't always happen, but it is natural for a young child to live in peace just as it is natural for a child of God to live in peace - in both instances, the mind is "stayed" or centered on the parent and his ways. Out of a simple, trusting relationship, the child centers its life on the parent. It is this uncomplicated atmosphere that is needed for the child to realize that he is truly loved by the parent and that it is good to return that love. It is in this relationship of giving and receiving love that a Christian can center his thinking on God all through the day - his mind is "stayed upon his heavenly Father Who keeps him in perfect peace. Perfect peace is without interruption - it is a continuing state of well-being. If we are to live in that kind of peace, we must pursue a continuing relationship that keeps our minds "stayed" on God.

To live in peace, we must be willing to do our part in our relationship with God. If we lose fellowship, our peace will fade. We have seen that Jesus is constantly knocking on the door of our heart - seeking to bring us into fellowship (Revelation 3:20). If we are willing to keep the door open, our relationship will be continuous, because God's love is with us all the time. Our minds will be centered or "stayed" upon God as we return His love.

The way to get serious about living in peace is to learn to return God's love, and we can do that by accepting His love. It is sometimes very difficult to accept God's love because of our pride and our tendency to seek worldly things. But when we humble ourselves and truly experience God's love, the result is amazing: His love makes us want to love Him in return. With a desire to love Him, it becomes natural to include Him in every circumstance during the day. In this way we can come to know Him- to trust Him and to truly love Him. We can look up to our heavenly Father with trust and adoration as small children sometimes do with their earthly parents.

It is really true - to love God is to have our mind "stayed" on Him, and to have our mind "stayed" on Him is to live in His peace. If we live in His peace, we will surely be at home with Him.

This figurative path that we have been following has led us to personal peace. This peace is in the midst of a loving relationship with our Father. If you think about it, I believe you will agree that this loving relationship is our spiritual home - the place where Christians can live in peace. The tragedy is that we tend to wander; we truly are like sheep that have gone astray - like sheep that need to come home. The path not only leads to personal peace; it leads home.

11
Come on Home

It is true that "the world is not our home," that "we are just passing through." A child of God could never make the world his home because the world does not possess spiritual life. Our spiritual home is in our relationship with God just as our human home is in our relationship with our family. We have seen that we lose our peace when we are not in relationship with God. Our personal peace depends upon our being at home with our heavenly Father.

But many of us are like a certain young man that left home because his Dad didn't let him have his own way. He gave up life with his family because he didn't want anybody to tell him what to do. That young man's actions put him in a position very much like most of us. We are separated from our heavenly Father because we don't want anybody telling us what to do. Many people decide against life with God by willfully going their own way. They are not conscious of their decision because they are absorbed in their activities. They just ignore God. They don't realize that they were created for fellowship and companionship and that it hurts God when they become indifferent to His loving concern. Like the parents of that young man, God's greatest desire is for them to come home.

People everywhere, many that go to church regularly, wonder why God is not more real to them. Some have acquired great knowledge of the Bible - some have even had an experience with Jesus Christ, but He is just not real anymore. Why? It is because they have gone their own way. The Bible says: "We are the ones who strayed away like sheep! We, who left God's paths to follow our own (way)" (Isaiah 53:6 LB). God wants us to be at home with Him, but many times we decide to leave because we love our own purposes in life instead of loving God.

Like the young man who gave up his family life, we all misuse our freedom to decide. Our Creator does not force us to do anything - He could have, but He did not create us to be robots. He loves us, and He wants us to love Him in return - a robot cannot do that. So we use our freedom of choice to make ourselves the center of life - to pursue our own purposes. We ignore God because we want to be our own God. Since there can be only one God, we are not comfortable in His presence. To follow our own way, we refuse to remain in the presence of the very One who created us. Outside God's presence, we can never have that personal relationship that is necessary to be at home with Him.

Without a personal relationship with God, there is no communication, no spiritual mooring, no peace. Like the young man that left home, there is no one to look to for love, wisdom, and strength. Life becomes complicated and heavy and sometimes burdensome. Into this dilemma, the words of Jesus come ringing down through the centuries: "Come unto me, all ye that labor and are heavy laden, and I will give you rest. Take my yoke upon you, and learn of me; for I am meek and lowly in heart: and ye shall find rest unto your souls" (Matthew 11:28, 29 KJV). His offer of rest for our souls is nothing less than personal peace. The graciousness and humility of our Lord is truly amazing - in response to our unfaithfulness, He sends out an invitation like that. Personal peace is available if we will yoke ourselves with Jesus (yoke is defined as a relationship such as marriage). He offers the kind of relationship that is found in the home - a relationship that is our spiritual home. He longs for us to stop "following our own way" - to come on home.

There is a grand old hymn that says: "I've wandered far away from God, now I'm coming home." Have you decided to stop wandering and come home to your heavenly Father? I have - first, with repentance; now, with great joy, I am coming home. As I walk with Him and talk with Him, He makes me know that He loves me and accepts me and wants me to be with Him. And the more I learn to love Him, the more I experience personal peace. I hope that it is the same with you. If you don't know that you love your heavenly Father, you can ask Him to help you to receive His love and then love Him in return. The few years that we call life is all the time we have to learn to live in God's peace - to be at home with Him. This is the time we have to be prepared for eternal life. If you have been wasting precious years, it's time - come on home.

Section II

GOING ON TO JOY

All of us, at some point in life, have wandered away from home with our heavenly Father. Just as our personal peace depends on our being at home with Him, our joy depends on our not wandering away from home (that relationship of knowing Him personally). When we stop wandering we can go on to great joy even if we are experiencing sorrow and pain in our lives.

Several years ago, I was pleasantly surprised to find that I had a gladness deep inside me that I could not explain. I was going through some very difficult times in my life and had been experiencing a lot of depression so I knew that God was doing a new thing in my life. I had been actively seeking answers in the scripture and the principles that I found there were making possible the joy that was coming out of my sorrow and pain. In section II then, let us look at these principles concerning joy and see how we can experience it every day of our lives.

Joy Out of Sorrow and Pain

For most of us, joy is a rather vague quality of life that sometimes seems elusive and hard to find. We all experience some degree of sorrow and pain in our lives and tend to reach for anything that resembles joy.

Depression, which is the opposite of joy, is so common in our society that it affects most of us to some degree - for many, it is a plague that causes heartache, and the inability to live life successfully. It is joy that is a necessary ingredient for success in life. Joy is the strength that is necessary to live life the way God intends for it to be lived. The scripture says "do not be grieved for the joy of the Lord is your strength". (Neh 8:10 b)

We don't think about strength or joy very much because, for most of us, happiness is the primary purpose in life. It becomes so important that we center our thinking and activity around the pursuit of things, people and the circumstances that we think will bring us happiness. Most people that gain a measure of happiness generally believe that they also have joy - the meaning of joy has become so vague that they confuse it with happiness not realizing that joy is a much more meaningful experience in life.

1
Happiness or Joy

Joy, unlike happiness, is not dependent on happenings or circumstances. A person in good health that has congenial company and pleasant surroundings may be happy but those circumstances in themselves do not bring joy. Joy comes from a confident expectation of all that is good and desirable in life. It is a gladness that comes out of an assurance that God is in control of a life that has been committed to Him - that He will make that person successful by developing in him talent and other qualities that are good and desirable. Joy is a glad assurance that God will work all things together for good. Of course, emotion can be a substitute, but real joy is more than emotion - it lies deep in the heart and comes only from God. (Ecc. 2:26) Real joy produces gladness, mental and emotional strength, satisfaction with life and a merry heart. In the Bible, it is described as the "fruit of God's Holy Spirit". (Gal. 5:22) Real joy is planted and made to grow by God if we depend upon Him to control our lives. Real joy, unlike happiness, can exist and even grow in the midst of sorrow and pain.

Our heavenly Father loves us very much, but He sometimes allows sorrow and pain in our lives. You may ask - why does a loving God permit sorrow and pain - why don't we have joy all the time? It is because He loves us and has a plan for each of our lives - a plan that requires our participation. He could have but He did not makes us robots. He has given us the privilege of choice - a free will. The problem is that we tend to ignore Him and seek to live life without His wisdom and guidance. Because our pride demands that we depend upon ourselves, we do not participate in God's plan for our lives - we devise our own plan. Then without His guidance, we sometimes allow our emotions to guide our lives. Left alone, they weave all sorts of unreal situations in our minds that upset us and cause emotional and even physical suffering. Many times in my life, suffering has caused me to see that I was ignoring God - that my pride was leading me away from His guidance and into sorrow and pain.

2
How Shall We React To Sorrow and Pain?

All of us, experience physical and emotional suffering as well as the sorrow and pain of accidents, disease and misfortune in our lives. The question is not whether we will suffer sorrow and pain. The question is: how will we react when suffering comes? Some people accept it and make it part of their lives. Others resent it and sometimes blame God. But the only valid way to react to suffering is to allow it to lead us into a closer relationship with our heavenly Father. Without a close relationship, we are strangers in God's house and do not have that expectation of all that is good and desirable.I believe that the glow of joy that we sometimes see on the little children's faces is a reflection of a confident expectation that their parents will meet all their needs. In the Christian life, it is in this kind of confident expectation that God produces joy - even in the midst of sorrow and pain. Well, you may ask - how can I have confident expectation so that I will have joy in my life? The answer is that the seed has already been planted even though it may be dormant in your heart. It is natural for a child to confidently expect its need to be met and it is the same in the spiritual realm. It is natural for a child of God to confidently expect our heavenly Father to give us all that is good and desirable in life. But if we allow guilt to separate us from Him, we cannot see the

reality of spiritual life and are not aware that
God has already placed confident expectation
deep in our hearts.

3
If Our Hearts Make us Feel Guilty

The Bible says in I John 3:21 (Amplified Bible) that if our hearts do not make us feel guilty, "we have confidence, complete assurance and boldness before God." That is certainly confident expectation but a person without it is allowing his heart to make him feel guilty. In the Bible, "the heart" is our conscience or the "attitude of our minds" and is shaped by our thinking. A person that allows his heart to make him feel guilty is accepting accusations from his own emotionally charged thinking in addition to the guilt that is the result of the circumstances of a life lived apart from God. Over time, the guilty thoughts begin to affect his thinking about himself that says: I am guilty. He may not admit it even to himself, but he already feels that he is guilty of not just one particular thing, but many things that he has stored up in his heart. This thought process is so subtle that it is not readily recognized. So for most people, the option of being forgiven is not even considered - they simply allow their hearts to make them feel guilty. The guilt may be real or imagined, but the result is always the same - they have no confidence before God because the guilt causes feelings of shame, anger and fear. When this happens their relationships with both God and man tend to become shallow because they are afraid to open their lives to others - they do not share their life with those around them for fear of being exposed by their guilt. Being open with others is considered to be a weakness and many live their lives around the idea of being "strong and silent". People in this dilemma tend to seek friends, wives and husbands that, like themselves, are afraid of deep relationships. This fear sometimes progresses to the point that they avoid and sometimes reject people that are willing to share their lives with others. It is a major problem in our society - people everywhere lose the confident expectation that God places in our hearts and that deprives them of joy. Their guilt and lack of joy hinders their relationships with their friends, with their marriage partners and with their God. But there is a way out - the way out, of course, is getting rid of the self-destructing attitude of guilt. But getting rid of guilt is not always easy. Because guilt adds to our separation from God, we become even more out of touch with the very One that has the solution. The solution for all guilt is God's forgiveness and he makes it available to all of us all the time. David said in Psalm 86:5 (RSV): "For thou, O Lord, art good and forgiving, abounding in steadfast love to all who call on thee".

4
Wiping The Slate Clean

God really does love us and wants us to have His forgiveness. If we receive it, our guilt is eliminated. If we are forgiven by God, we cannot be guilty anymore! Of course, it is good to have the forgiveness of men, but God's forgiveness "wipes the slate clean" because He is the one we are ultimately responsible to. He will eliminate all of our guilt if we are willing to call upon Him for forgiveness. That probably sounds like an easy solution, but for most of us, it is difficult because our pride demands that we depend upon ourselves. Because of that, many people will not even consider their guilt or their need for forgiveness. Our minds are capable of devising hundreds of ways to keep us from seeing the reality of our guilt. We become our own enemy by refusing to see our need for forgiveness - we unwittingly choose to remain guilty and forfeit the confident expectation that is the source of joy.

It has been said that "humanity is never so beautiful as when praying for forgiveness or offering forgiveness to others". Giving and receiving forgiveness leads to joy and joy changes things - it makes humanity beautiful. But the benefits of joy will never be yours unless you are both giving and receiving forgiveness. The same pride that refuses to see our need for forgiveness refuses to forgive the things others do that hurt us. If we are to have joy in our lives, we must put down pride and be willing to forgive and be forgiven.

"Whenever you stand praying, if you have anything against anyone, forgive him and let it drop - leave it - let it go - in order that your Father who is in heaven may also forgive you your failings and shortcomings and let them drop. But if you do not forgive, neither will your Father in heaven forgive your failings and shortcomings". (Mark 11:25-26 Amplified) That is a direct quotation from the words of Jesus and it contains the key to a joy filled life. The obstacle of guilt is eliminated by God's forgiveness but we must forgive to be forgiven.

Jesus is saying in this verse, that our forgiving others makes it possible to receive forgiveness for ourselves - it says that "in order that your Father who is in heaven may also forgive you." He wants us to have all the forgiveness we need but He cannot give it to us if we are not close enough to Him to receive it. If we resent and refuse to forgive others we are hating them and hate makes us guilty before God. We have already seen that guilt separates us from God and makes communication through a personal relationship with Him impossible. Without this communication, it is not possible to receive His forgiveness - to be forgiven by God or anyone else, we must be in close touch with them. But if we put down pride and are willing to forgive others and receive forgiveness for ourselves, we have a new relationship with our heavenly Father - a relationship in which He can and will forgive us. Then His Holy Spirit gives us the strength to overcome the arguments of our minds that convince us that we are not resentful or unforgiving. If we renounce resentment and the critical attitude that accompanies it, the circumstances of our lives take on a new reality. It then becomes evident that the guilt of resentment and other sin in our lives has robbed us of the communication we need with our heavenly Father - communication through a personal relationship that makes it possible to receive His forgiveness and His joy.

5
New Life From God

The scripture says, in 1 John 1:9, that if we confess our sins to God, (talking to him personally) that He will forgive us and cleanse us from all unrighteousness. He forgives us and wipes away all of our guilt if we come into relationship with Him and tell Him that we know that we have been wrong - that we want to receive the forgiveness and cleansing that was made possible when Jesus paid the penalty for our sin with His death on the cross. God's forgiveness and cleansing is the very thing that is necessary to be born into the family of God - to be "born again". When we turn away from sin, believing that Jesus has already paid the penalty for it, we can receive the very life of God. We are born spiritually when we truly receive Jesus and His forgiveness into our hearts and lives. With new life from God, we can go on to be cleansed from unrighteousness - we become more and more righteous. That is, we have more and more "right standing" - the right to stand before our heavenly Father. Then, with this new relationship, our hearts do not make us feel guilty anymore - we have confidence, complete assurance and boldness before God - - we have confident expectation. We can confidently expect all that is good and desirable in life and know that God will work all things together for good as we fit into His plan for our lives. Out of this, God's Holy Spirit produces the fruit of joy regardless of the circumstances.

6
Sorrow, Pain And the Fruit called Joy

Sorrow and pain may be present at various times in our lives, but joy has the capacity to cover the suffering with mental and emotional strength. Then we can actually be glad for the suffering as we see God developing in us new talent, strength of character as well as mental, emotional and spiritual maturity - the things that are necessary to be the best we can be in this life. In addition, He very often changes difficult circumstances in ways that turn suffering into blessing. If we nourish the confident expectation of these and other blessings, joy will be present even in the midst of sorrow and pain. Over time, if we continue in this, it is possible to experience joy every day of our lives as we discipline our minds to expect the best from God. What we are talking about is living a normal Christian life, but it cannot be lived by standing on the sidelines without a personal relationship with our Lord. We must stop conforming our thinking to the negative things in the world around us. We must discover the good and desirable things that God has in store for us and talk to Him about the way He wants to fit them into our lives. Through a close personal relationship, we can stand before God with confident expectancy day by day. When that is done over a period of time, joy begins to ripen into the precious fruit that it is - the fruit of God's Holy Spirit.

Section III

GOING ON TO LOVE WITHOUT FEAR

We have seen that joy, like personal peace, is part of the fruit of God's Holy Spirit. But that fruit is not available to us if we allow fear to defeat our loving relationships with God and with men. Fear threads its way through all of our relationships to one degree or another. If our personal relationships are to work for our good, we need to love others fearlessly - more than that, as we shall see, fearless love is absolutely necessary if we are going to get to know God personally.

Fearless Love

Love or the lack of it probably occupies more of a man's attention than any single thing in life - it is a basic need. It may be love for family, for friends, or for God; but all of us, to some degree, are both drawn by a desire for it and repelled by a fear of it. We are either open or closed to loving relationships but all of us instinctively know that we need an answer concerning this great need for love in our lives. It is what we do about this need that determines the course of our lives and whether we live a life that has meaning.

1
The Purpose of Life

Why do we have such a need to love and be loved? It is because God is love and "He has made us in His likeness" (Gen. 1:26). We are to have love for God and man growing out of God's love for us. All of human existence is built around love because God wants to prepare us to live with Him forever. But this does not take place as long as we just let life happen - living life according to our own ways - guided by our own self-interest. The Bible calls this sin. But when we set aside our own ways (repent) and accept forgiveness for our sin, Jesus gives us His kind of life-spiritual life-we are "born again." But that is only the beginning. This world is a place that God has placed us in to get to know Him as we receive this forgiveness of sin that was made possible by Jesus' death on the cross. It is here that He gives us time to develop a loving relationship with Him which will not end with physical death, but will last forever. If we are going to live life according to God's purpose, we simply must be in relationship with Him and let Him use the time we have in this life to not only make us successful here but to prepare us for life hereafter. If we are to do this, we must let the human need that we have for love lead us to a greater need - the need for a loving relationship with our heavenly Father. Let us then look at human relationships and then look at the kind of relationships that God wants for us.

As much as we glamorize and idealize human love, it is not adequate in real life. To some degree, our self-interest enters in so that our love is always mixed with the fear of being hurt. You may ask - why does my love have to do with fear? Well, you can answer that yourself - think of the times your thoughts were dominated by the feeling that someone had treated you unfairly or had not returned the love you offered them or had abused you as a child or any of the life experiences all of us have that wound us emotionally. Does that not make us fearful of trusting others with our love? I believe that everyone of us is affected in some way by the hurtful experiences that cause fear and mistrust. Because of this element of fear, love to some degree, is withheld from everyone we encounter - even those closest to us. But more damaging than that, love is withheld from God. If we withhold our love from Him, we cannot grow into that loving relationship that is necessary for us to live with Him forever. For many years, I withheld love for God without really knowing it. I knew that Jesus said that the most important commandment is to "love the Lord thy God with all thy heart and with all thy soul and with all thy mind" (Matt 22:37). But for me, it was as though being a Christian meant that I automatically loved God. Because I wanted to obey the command to love Him I assumed that I did. I did not realize that my fear kept me from truly giving myself to Him. There is a fine line between wanting to love someone and actually giving them our love - that fine line is fear. I did not realize that my fear was depriving me of the only real solution for my hurting emotions - that solution was a loving relationship with my heavenly Father.

2
What are Personal Relationships?

If we are to have abundant life here and in the life to come, we must be through with fear and open ourselves to loving relationships with both God and men. Think for a minute what a personal or loving relationship actually is. Is it not simply receiving someone's love and then loving them in return? That's the way it always begins, whether the relationship is with God or family or friends. But a relationship does not survive unless both persons continue to give and receive love. if either person begins to withhold love, the relationship begins to die. That is why personal relationships in our society are so fragile - one or both persons become fearful of being hurt emotionally and withdraw. Then feelings are hurt and many times one or both feel rejected. Then pride rears its ugly head and each one rejects the other simply because they feel they have been rejected. The anger that comes out of this always leads to an unforgiving attitude. All of us have faults that need to be forgiven; but, if the other person is angry, he is unwilling to forgive - this makes a loving relationship impossible because forgiveness is a basic ingredient of love.

The failure in relationships that I have been describing may not apply to you directly; but, if you think about it, I think you will agree that all of us are sometimes guilty of unforgiveness - sometimes in subtle ways that hide our failure to forgive. On the other hand, many say that they have a right to be resentful or unforgiving, not realizing that it is an expression of hate. We are told again and again in the scripture to forgive but most of us sometimes engage in the morbid self-gratification that we politely call resentment.

3
The Cycle of Fear

Resentment is unforgiveness and, when it continues, it dominates our thinking and becomes a critical attitude which is hostile. Hostility generally causes a hostile response which causes more anger and fear. What we are talking about is a vicious cycle that affects all of us to some degree. It begins with fear and ends with more fear. It begins with fear of emotional hurt which causes us to reject others which causes anger, resentment (unforgiveness) and a critical attitude. The cycle ends in more fear because a critical attitude is hostile and we realize the possibility of a hostile response by the other person.

You may say that you are not fearful and that none of this applies to you, but can you say that you always accept everyone just as they are and forgive everything they say or do that is wrong? Do you always offer love without reservation? Can you say you never engage in subtle words or deeds that are really a substitute for genuine love in certain situations? I think you will agree that all of us get caught up in some part of the cycle of fearful love from time to time - not only with men but also with God. The real question is: how can we be through with this cycle of fearful love and enter into a cycle of fearless love?

We have already seen some of the ways that fear destroys relationships. But suppose fear was eliminated - would not each person be willing to accept the other's love and would not each person willingly offer their own love? I think so - they would be free to love because there would be no fear. Well that is all very fine, but how can fear be eliminated? The answer is in the cycle itself. A cycle is like a ring or a circle; but in motion, it is a process that ends where it begins - it completes itself and becomes a perfect circle or cycle. Relationships are like that - they are completed or perfected each time each person gives and then receives love - they become perfect in their completion. The Bible says in 1 John 4:18 that "There is no fear in love, but perfect love cast our fear." There is the key! When the cycle is completed or made perfect, fear is cast out - eliminated. Fear cannot remain in the presence of perfect love. As each person continues to give and receive love, fear drops away and the relationship begins to grow and mature. The kind of relationship God wants us to have with Him and with each other comes out of a cycle of fearless love.

4
The Cycle of Fearless Love

Fearless love is not fragile because it is not willing to withdraw. A person with this kind of love goes on loving even if the other person withdraws and becomes indifferent or hostile. Jesus said in Luke 6:27 and 28: "Love your enemies, do good to those that hate you, bless those who curse you and pray for those who abuse you." This may seem difficult at first, but it shows that God expects us to continue to love no matter what. Just think of the strength and stability in that kind of love - it does not withdraw - it is fearless love in action. But when I read those verses, I know that I cannot love like that out of my human resources. None of us can love fearlessly without a measure of God's love. It is only when we participate in that cycle of fearless love with our heavenly Father that we can love others whether they are our enemy or just a neighbor. If we are receiving God's love, we can love Him in return and love others the way He wants us to love them.

5
An Anchor of Love

We have seen that fear drops away as love is being given and received, but how do we get into this cycle of fearless love? Most of us need to be loved before we can love - the more fearful we are, the more we need to be reassured by another's love. But many times we are too fearful to accept another's love when it is offered to us. It is no wonder that relationships are so fragile in our society - people tend to wait on each other to commit themselves and even when a relationship begins, they tend to depend on the other to keep the cycle going. But there is a way out of this dilemma. In ! John 4:19, it says that we can love because God loves us first. His love is so powerful that it meets the need we have to become a loving people. Our need is to possess the love of someone that never withdraws - that keeps on loving us no matter what we do. That is exactly the kind of love God offers us. God's love can give us the assurance that is necessary to enter into the cycle of fearless love with Him and with our neighbors. If we receive His love, we willingly complete or perfect that love by loving Him in return. Then perfect love casts out fear and we are not only able to love God, but we are then able to love our neighbors even if they are not loving us. Our heavenly Father would not command us to love Him and our neighbor if He were not making it possible. He makes it possible with His gift of never-ending love - a love that He will never withdraw. We can hold on to God's love when others are not loving us - His love is an anchor in any relationship. If others withdraw or become indifferent toward us, we can depend on God's love - it is always there. When anyone begins to depend on God's love for an anchor, it becomes easier to get to know Him; and when anyone truly knows God, there is a conviction, a personal "knowing," that His infallible love is eternal and will never be withdrawn. With this conviction, we can love others in a fearless way and we can keep on loving them as long as we are depending on God's love as an anchor. But that anchor is not available unless we get to know Him and receive His love.

6
Getting to Know God

Most of us know about God, but how many of us really know Him as a person? We surely must know about Him before we can get to know Him, but it is in getting to know Him that we are able to trust Him enough to enter into that cycle of fearless love. We must know Him in His humility, in His patience, and in His kindness; but most of all, we must know Him in His forgiveness. As we draw closer, we see the great difference between His sinless nature and our own nature - we become acutely aware of our sin and our need for forgiveness. Out of this awareness, we can begin to receive God's love by receiving the forgiveness that He offers us so freely. The scripture says that "If we confess our sins to Him, He can be depended on to forgive us and to cleanse us" (1 John 1:9 LB). Sin is basically living our way instead of God's way - all of us have a continuing need to confess this and receive forgiveness. God's forgiveness is part of His gift of never-ending love, but we must reach out and receive it - something offered never becomes a gift until it is received. If we are to receive God's love, we must begin by receiving His forgiveness because unforgiven sin separates us from Him. If we don't deliberately receive God's gift of forgiveness, we are still guilty of the sin that separates us and a personal relationship with Him is impossible. We must deliberately confess all past and present sin - then, day by day, we must confess the sin in our thought life. Jesus said that evil thoughts proceed out of our hearts and defile us (Matt 15:19-20 RSV). But when we confess these thoughts. He forgives us and cleanses us from sin. If we accept His gift of forgiveness, we have the key to life because we are actively receiving His love. Then a personal relationship becomes a reality as we return His love. In the latter part of Luke 7:47, Jesus expresses this as a spiritual principle while forgiving a repentant prostitute. He said, "He who is forgiven little, loves little." The corollary to this would be that he who is forgiven much, loves much. It is really true - the more of God's loving forgiveness we receive, the more we are able to fearlessly give our own love - His loving forgiveness is the key that opens our heart. That sounds simple enough, but pride makes it difficult to openly and genuinely receive a gift from another person - even God's gift of forgiveness. Without humility, our pride develops in us a need to be deserving of anything we receive from others. But if we humble ourselves, we are able to receive this gift from God - the forgiveness of sin. The scripture says that it is our responsibility to humble ourselves - it says in 1 Peter 5:5&6: "God opposes the proud but gives grace to the humble. Humble yourselves therefore under the mighty hand of God." This is sometimes difficult for most of us, but humility becomes easier as we get to know God in His humility - the God of the Universe is a humble person. It helps me to see the humility of God, and know that it is ridiculous for me, the created, to be proud while the creator, who is so superior, is a humble person. That helps me to put pride down, and receive this great gift of forgiveness.

7
We Must Open the Door

When we openly receive God's forgiveness, the burden of sin is lifted and there is a new freedom to fellowship with Him. Being free from the guilt of sin is such a blessed thing that thankfulness wells up from deep down inside and ignites a desire to give love to the One who sets us free - he who is forgiven much, loves much. Then with praise and thanksgiving, we begin to return God's love. By returning His love, we complete it or make it perfect - then fear is eliminated. When fear is eliminated, we are free to enter into that cycle of fearless love - first with our heavenly Father - then with our neighbor. When we enter into this fearless love with God, we open the door to a whole new life with Him. Being in fellowship with Him makes it possible for Him to teach us - to mold us and make us to be like Jesus - to prepare us to live with Him forever. The problem is that we become more interested in receiving blessings for our physical lives than the spiritual blessings that are in God's plan for all of us. It is His will that we seek spiritual blessing first - Jesus said, "Seek ye first the Kingdom of God and His righteousness and all these things shall be added unto you" (Matt 6:33 KJV). Seeking God first is entirely foreign to many of us - our physical needs seem so important. We become so involved in our physical lives that we not only fail to seek God, we are unaware that He is seeking us. In Revelation 3:20, our Lord makes this astounding statement: "I have been standing at the door and I am constantly knocking. If anyone hears me calling him and opens the door, I will come in and fellowship with him and he with me." This fellowship, of course, comes in the process of giving love to God and receiving love from Him. He seeks that for us and for Himself, but it depends upon hearing His knock and His voice as He calls us.

Many of us are so caught up in the affairs of this physical life that we are unable to hear the voice of the One that placed us on this earth. All of us have a great need to hear God - allowing Him to speak to us through the scripture and by placing His thoughts in our minds - but more than that, we need to hear His "still small voice" calling us. We need to open the door of our hearts so that we can have that close communication with Him that we call fellowship. We need communication with Him all through the day - allowing Him to speak to us in as many ways as He chooses and responding to Him as the Holy Spirit enables us to pray - prayer is simply talking to God. As the Holy Spirit gives us the "very words to pray," the relationship is complete - the door of our heart is open and Jesus comes in to fellowship. We are hearing God and being heard by Him - that is communication. This communication with our Lord makes possible the preparation we need to live this life and life hereafter. If we fearlessly give and receive love in fellowship with God, we will want to love those that He loves - we will want to love our neighbor and

ourselves; then through the power of His Holy
Spirit, that begins to happen - not with our
inadequate human love, but with the love we
receive from God. We become a channel for
His Love as His love is "poured into our hearts
through the Holy Spirit" (Rom. 5:5). When that
happens, we begin to take on the very
character of God - we become more and more
like Jesus. It is God's plan that the time we
have on this earth be used to become like Him
so that we can live with Him forever. That
means that we must not only love God with all
of our heart, mind and soul, but we must love
our neighbor even as we love ourselves.

It is vital that all of us adopt this plan that
God has for our lives. There are so many that
live out their lives not even knowing why they
are here. I hope that is not true of you - I hope
that you have accepted the key to life and
have fearlessly opened the door of your heart
to our loving Lord - that you fellowship with
Him to the degree that you know that peace
that "passes all understanding" and that you
have the calm assurance that God, is truly
preparing you for eternal life with Him. If that
is not true of you, it can be - our Lord is
constantly knocking on the door of your heart.
He is always right there seeking us out because
He created us for fellowship. All through the
scripture, it is evident that He earnestly desires
for us to enter into loving fellowship with
Him. There is a grand old hymn that talks
about this - it says:

The Savior is waiting to enter your heart
Why don't you let Him come in
There's nothing in this world
to keep you apart
What is your answer to Him.
Time after time He has waited before
And now He is waiting again
To see if you are willing
To open the door
Oh, how He wants to come in.

My prayer is that you will not stop when you make a profession of faith and become a church member - even a church leader - that is only the beginning. Our Lord has given to us the key to life - His never-ending love. We must accept it and fearlessly go on to open the door of our hearts and enter into fellowship - a loving relationship with the One that loves us so. That is what a Christian is - someone that has fellowship with God- someone that is in the process of receiving all that our loving heavenly Father has for us in this life and the life to come.

Section IV

GOING THROUGH HINDRANCE TO VICTORY

We have come a long way in this journey to knowing God personally and yet there remains a hindrance that all of us must overcome. It is so easy to talk about fearlessly opening the door of our hearts and receiving God's love but this life we have in the flesh is very much against that. The flesh, left to itself, is not humble enough to receive love from God. In this section we will see the way through this hindrance - a way that leads to victory in the Christian life.

Receiving God's Love

1
Human Love or God's Love

Today all over America, to one degree or another, devastation occurs in families and individual lives because all of us tend to offer human love in our personal relationships. But it is God's love that produces the fruit of the Holy Spirit which is joy, peace, long suffering, kindness, goodness, faithfulness, gentleness and self control (Gal. 5:22 & 5:23.) Any one of these qualities is worth more than any price we could ever pay. Can you imagine a marriage or any personal relationship breaking down if these qualities are present? Many people expend a lot of energy in a great show of human love but if they are not giving God's love, the relationship breaks down. The result is indifference, quarrels, divorce, crime and on the national level, bad foreign relations and even war. Only God's love works in this life. If it is not God's love given through His children, it is just not real. And if it is not real, it becomes a show in which we are the play actors. People everywhere spend much of their time and energy starring in a play written and directed by themselves. The play is generally about giving and receiving love - human love. The reason humanity gives and receives human love is because most people have not received God's love - we cannot give something we do not have. It is vital in all of our lives that we receive God's love so that we

can love Him back and love those around us
with His love.

2
Accepting From Others

If you are a Christian, the fact that God gives you His love is not new to you. What may be new is that you have to accept it (receive it) or it will not become yours. Suppose someone holds a new watch out to you - a loving gift. That watch will never be yours until you reach out and accept it and make it your own. If you think about it, that is true of any gift - especially the gift of God's loving forgiveness. The essence of salvation is receiving God's forgiveness which is part of His love. So all Christians begin by receiving His love. But to grow up in the Christian life, we must continue to receive His loving forgiveness because we continue to sin. When we receive His love, we receive Him because He is love (1 John 4:8). When we receive Him, we can become victorious over sin. Jesus paid the price for our sin with His life but that was not the end of it - He was raised up (resurrected) by the power of the Holy Spirit. With His death, forgiveness of sin became available to anyone who asks for it with a repentant heart. With His resurrection, He provided victory over our future sin - when we receive Jesus, we receive His resurrected life which is eternal and very powerful. His bloody death on that cross and His resurrected life from the grave provide us complete victory over all sin as we receive Him. When we receive Him, we are "born again" - not physical birth but spiritual birth - the very life of

God. With this new life we have the power to do what He wants us to do which includes the power to obey His command to forgive those who have offended us. when we do that, we are able to receive more of His forgiveness. The more forgiveness we receive, the more of Him we receive and the more of Him we receive the more we are filled with His Holy Spirit. The Holy Spirit then gives us the power of His resurrected life (Acts 1:8). The love begins to appear in the form of spiritual fruit which is part of our Lord's plan for our lives. But all this is possible only as we receive more and more of God's forgiving love. Then as we begin to return His love, we have a personal relationship with Him.

3
Abiding In The Vine

Some of the things Jesus said about relationships were: "Receive Me," "Abide in Me," "Come into union with Me as I am in Union with the Father" and then He said that the greatest commandment is "You shall love the Lord your God with all your heart, with all your soul, and with all your mind" (Matt. 22:37.) That is a very close personal relationship. It is clear that He wants us to be more than a casual acquaintance - He wants us to abide in His love just as a branch abides in a vine. If a Christian, who is a branch, abides in Jesus, the Vine, through a loving relationship, he comes into union with Him and with our heavenly Father. The branch then produces the fruit of the Holy Spirit - joy, peace, long suffering, kindness, goodness, faithfulness, gentleness and self control. We then, to a degree, have these qualities in common with God and they become the basis of an even deeper relationship with our Lord (John chapter 15). It is exciting to know that the God of the universe wants to build us up in His grace to the point that we can be that close to Him. He actually makes it possible for us to obey the "greatest commandment" as we receive His love. But there is one thing we must do before that can happen and that is to humble ourselves (Mic. 6:8). Over and over the Bible says that we must humble ourselves. In 1 Pet. 5:6 it says: "Humble yourselves under the mighty hand of God."

4
Humility

It is not possible for our hearts to receive anything or anybody if we have not first humbled ourselves. it is true that receiving another's love promotes humility but we must have a measure of humility to begin a loving relationship. In the Bible, born again believers are called the bride of Christ - so the physical example that God has given us is marriage. In this life, marriage is never consummated unless the bride receives the physical love of her husband. In trusting humility, she receives him and they come into union with each other. That is exactly what Jesus wants for us. We, the bride of Christ, are to come into union with Him as He is in union with the Father (John 17:21). This, of course is spiritual union but the principle is the same - union that is physical or spiritual, if it is genuine, must begin with humility. Humility is absolutely necessary to receive God's love but He would never pressure us to be humble. If today you were forced to be humble, you would become a robot because you would no longer have a will of your own. I think you will agree that it is not possible for a robot to enter a loving relationship. Receiving love from another is something we must will to do in our hearts - we must put aside the love and concern we have for ourselves to make room for the love of another. God's love is all around us all the time - if we make room, He will surely come in.

5
Controlling The Ego

You may ask: how can I control this ego of mine and humble myself so that I can receive God's love. In his classic book, *The Imitation of Christ*, Thomas a' Kempis puts it like this: "Never desire to be singularly praised or loved; for this belongs to God alone, who has none like Himself. Neither desire that anyone's heart should be taken up with you; nor be you much taken up with the love of anyone; but let Jesus be in you and in every good man." That is the exact opposite of the desire of the ego. Every one of us since the fall of Adam want to play God on our own private stage. Our ego doesn't want to be dependent on anyone, it wants others to be dependent on us. But there is only one who is not dependent on anyone and that is God. We want to be praised and loved as somebody special even to the extent that others hearts are so taken up with us that they will be so dependent on us that we will be "like God." Satan tempted Eve and then Adam with the idea that they could be "like God" (Gen. 3:4&5). If we were like God, then we would be alike or equal to the One who created us. The truth is: we were created in the image of God (Gen. 1:27). We are to be a reflection of Him - to be more and more like Him. That is far different than being equal to Him. We live in a society that compete among ourselves to be somebody special. In the course of that competition, it is decided who will lead and who will follow. The followers commit themselves to the leaders expecting to be part of a group that is "something special." Even though they are followers, they are part of the rebellion against God that began with the first man Adam. They satisfy themselves with the idea that they are part of a group that is special ("like God") and therefore they are somebody special. This desire to be singularly praised and loved simply must be controlled in our lives because singular praise or special praise and love belong to one person and one person only - God.

Most of us lacked humility when we began our new life in Christ. For years I was totally lacking in humility - I simply modified my thinking and my behavior and began producing my own stage play. Much later, I began to understand that we are a new creation and that old things are to pass away and all things are to become new (2 Cor. 5:17). If we continue to modify our old sin nature instead of controlling it, we will still have that desire to be "like God." As long as we allow that desire to remain, we will actually be God's competitor and not His subject. He is the King and if we want to receive the love of the King, we must humble ourselves.

As we humble ourselves, our faith rises and we become more dependent on God. We are then able to give up the desire to control people and circumstances which had been necessary to gain the status of somebody special or part of a special group. Life then becomes more real and we see ourselves in a new and better way - not fearing what men may say but striving to please God who loves us so. It is said that a humble person does not stoop smaller than he is; he stands at his real height seeing the reality of how small he is compared to God. When he humbles himself, he does not have to put on an act anymore because he has the real thing. He, of course, is opposed by those who do not have the real thing and experiences some form of persecution - such as a loss of friends. Jesus said: "if they persecuted Me, they will also persecute you." But humility causes us to begin to fit into God's Kingdom and into the purpose He has for our lives which is fellowship with Himself. In trusting humility, we can open the door of our heart to Jesus Himself and consummate our spiritual marriage to Him through a real, personal, loving relationship (Rev. 3:20).

6
An Exchange of Love

Simply put, any relationship is an exchange of love - the giving and receiving of love. Our Lord makes this exchange possible through the power of His love that He offers us continually. The Bible says that we can love God because He first loved us (1 John 4:19). Jesus holds His love out to us 24 hours of every day - He is that available. We can receive His love anytime simply by humbly opening the door of our heart. Then through the power of His love, we have the strength to overcome our old sin nature and love Him back. Because He loves us first, we are able to do our part and complete an exchange of love. This exchange of love is similar to human relationships, but it is so much more. We, the branches, out of this union with Jesus, the Vine, can now produce the the fruit of the Holy Spirit - joy, peace, long suffering, kindness, etc. It is these qualities that tie us together with our Lord in eternal fellowship. Through this close personal relationship, we can have loving companionship and that peace "that passes all understanding" now and throughout eternity - that is something to shout about!

Section V

GOING ON TO THE ABUNDANCE IN LIFE

Many people are not aware of the great abundance that is available to all of us in this life. It is available because our heavenly Father loves each one of us with great and powerful love - a love which, if received, actually creates the physical and spiritual abundance that we all need in life.

As we have seen, receiving God's love has been a problem for man almost from the beginning. The abundance that accompanies God's love has always been available, but because it is available does not mean we have it - we can have it only as we receive it. To go on to abundance - to be fruitful in our Christian lives, we must receive more and more from our heavenly Father.

Living More Abundantly

Abundance in this life is not for just a privileged few; it is yours and mine for the taking. Some time ago, I found a key that opened a whole new way of life for me - a life that is becoming more and more abundant. My desire had been for an abundance of material things. I had not seen the reality of the spiritual need that I had, to live life "more abundantly"."More abundantly" was the way Jesus described the spiritual life that He came to offer us. He said that it was His purpose to give us life and give it to us more abundantly. (John 10:10). Like most people, I did not realize that physical abundance is less valuable than spiritual abundance; that, with spiritual abundance, our material needs are taken care of by God. Jesus said, "Seek first the kingdom of God and His righteousness, and all these things shall be added to you." (Matthew 6:33). Most of us seek "things" or physical abundance first. All of us need to seek spiritual abundance first - then the "things" or physical abundance will be added. But, more than that, we need to allow God to prepare us to live with Him in eternity. In the process, we will know abundance spiritually and physically.

What I would like to talk about, then, is the spiritual principles that can lead all of us into a life that is more abundant. We shall see that living life more abundantly is dependent on how much we love with God's kind of love, and that depends on how much of His love we are willing to receive. There is the key' we simply are not able to truly love anyone until we begin to receive that great love that our heavenly Father has for each of us individually.

All of us, in one way or another, seek to be loved. Yet, we are hesitant to accept it when offered for fear of being hurt. Without knowing it, we are seeking a love that will never be withdrawn; the very kind of love that God offers to us. Many people are not aware that God loves them just the way they are, and that He will continue to love them regardless of what they have done. All through the Bible

God invites us to experience His great love now and forever. He says He loves us with an "everlasting love." (Jeremiah 31:3) His mercy, compassion, and loving kindness are available to us every moment throughout all eternity. That is the kind of love we can depend on in the storms of life - it is the anchor we need to bring stability in our lives. In addition, God's love is the ever-present source of joy and peace. It is the strength we need to live this life more abundantly.

I think it is safe to say that a person is never the same after receiving God's love. The Bible says that old things pass away and all things become new - that a person becomes a new creature as he receives God's forgiveness (which is God's love in action). Of course, that kind of change takes place only as we realize how separated we are from God and how desperately we need His forgiveness for ignoring Him and going our own way. In going our own way, we say things and do things that separate us from Him. But, it is not only the things we say and do, it is the resentment, anger, envy, lust, jealousy, and all the other sinful thoughts that occupy our minds. For most of us, the majority of our sin happens in our mind. Jesus said that it is our thought life that pollutes us and makes us unfit for God. (Mark 7:20-23). If we allow sinful thoughts to remain in our minds, we sin. The Bible says, "As he (anyone) thinketh in his heart, so is he." As I ponder that, the reality of my sin comes home to me. Our very character is determined by the kind of thinking we allow in our minds. Our thought life can, and does, cause us to sin. The scripture says that all of us sin and fall short of what God expects of us. That means that all of us have a great need to accept God's loving forgiveness. But, even though He constantly offers us this gift of loving forgiveness, we will never have it if we do not accept it. I think you would agree that something offered does not become a gift until it is received.

1
Receiving From God

People everywhere, many who are regular church-goers, wonder why God is not more real to them. Some have had an experience with Jesus Christ, but He is just not real to them. Why? It is because they never really received His loving forgiveness down deep inside where the guilt is. It is the guilt of following our own way that bends and distorts life and keeps us from receiving the abundance that God wants to give to each of us. Without realizing it, we allow this guilt to affect our thinking. We become uneasy because of this underlying and sometimes unconscious guilty feeling. If the guilt is not resolved, it has devastating effects. It causes us to blame ourselves and others for any number of things which causes emotional pains like worry, anxiety and a loss of self-confidence. Then, in order to get rid of the pain, we begin to blame those around us - we try to transfer the guilt which, to one degree or another, turns us against others. Then we become fearful and angry and then resentful and critical of others - it is a cycle that takes us down and down without our even knowing it. This cycle very often ends in depression and sometimes self-pity. That certainly is not the abundant life Jesus promised us - it is the sin that so easily besets us. (Hebrews 12:1). This cycle of guilt besets us, or defeats us, because we do not know it is happening. Martin Luther said, "The ultimate proof of the sinner is that he does not know his own sin." But, we can know it and recognize it for what it is - it is the cycle that begins with the guilt of wanting to live life without regard for what God has said and ends with either worry, anger, resentment, loneliness or depression or a combination of all of them. But there is a solution - a very simple one. The only real solution for this guilt cycle is forgiveness - God's forgiveness. We need to have forgiveness from other people, but they are not our Judge - God is. Without His loving forgiveness, we can never function successfully in this life. It is impossible to be guilty if you have truly received forgiveness from God who is the judge. He has provided this loving gift in Jesus Christ, His Son, who died for your sin and mine. But, the guilt will not leave you unless you receive this loving forgiveness into the very depths of your being. If you are not sure you have done this, I hope you will do it now. You can begin to receive God's love by receiving His forgiveness. The scripture says, "If we confess our sins, He is faithful and just to forgive us our sins and to cleanse us from all unrighteousness." (1 John 1:9). Simply tell our heavenly Father that you know that you are sinful, that you know that when Jesus died and rose again, the penalty for your sin was paid - that you know that you do not have to be guilty anymore - that you want to be forgiven and cleansed from this cycle of guilt and sin. Remember that we are responsible for all known sin, including resentment and the deep-seated anger that accompanies it. Be sure to confess that to our heavenly Father. Then ask Him for His loving forgiveness and receive it into the very core of your being. Welcome it into your heart knowing that you have complete and total forgiveness. Then, on the authority of God's word, you can feel secure in the knowledge that this forgiveness will always be available to you as you confess any future sin - guilt will never devastate your life again. With the barrier of guilt out of the way, you can begin to let Him speak to you, to guide you, to love you. As we let Him love us, we are able to love Him in return. Having shed the burden of guilt, we are free to return His love and enter into a personal relationship with our heavenly Father.

2
Personal Relationships

Basically, a personal relationship with God is very similar to a personal relationship with a friend, a husband, a wife, or any other person. It is simply an exchange of love - a giving and receiving of love between persons. There was a time in my life that God was more like a thing than a person simply because we can not see Him while in this physical body. But, I came to see that He is a tender loving person who loves me personally. In fact, you and I are persons because He is a person. The scripture says that we are "made in His likeness". (Genesis 1:26). He made us like Himself for a reason - He wants a people or a family that will receive His love and love Him in return. The very purpose of our existence is to fellowship with our heavenly Father - to develop a personal relationship with Him. To state that so simply, almost takes away from the glorious meaning that it has for our lives. But, it is true; the intent of our heavenly Father is to develop a relationship with each of us that is greater than anything we could ever have with family or friends here on earth. The best of loving relationships that we have here on earth is only an example of what God wants for us in His family. He has set us in families here and now so that He can prepare us to live in His family in eternity. All of this physical life is simply a way that God has to prepare us for everlasting life with Him.

All through the Bible, we see God's yearning for His people to accept His love and love Him in return. He says that "He cares for us", that He will "wipe away all our tears", as we come to Him. That means we can be through with all of our anger, resentment and fear. It means that we don't have to be lonely or depressed; that we can have companionship that we never dreamed possible. It means that life can be more satisfying and more fulfilling - we can live more abundantly. Then, as we share our life with the One who has such a great love for us, He begins to challenge us to fulfill the plan that He has for our lives. (Ephesians 2:10). If we respond to this challenge, life takes on purpose and meaning as we unite with Him in a personal relationship. At this point, the effect of God's love is nothing short of profound, because we begin to receive the fullness and power of God's Holy Spirit.

3
Spirit-Filled Abundance

We simply cannot live more abundantly without the fullness of the Holy Spirit. And, we cannot be "Spirit-filled" until we come into union with God the Father and Jesus Christ His Son through an exchange of love. The scripture says that "God has given us the Holy Spirit to fill our hearts with His love." (Romans 5:5). This is not just an emotional experience that He gives us - He gives us Himself - the Holy Spirit. When we receive this love, we receive the Holy Spirit - we cannot receive one without the other. Each time we open our heart and receive His love, we experience an indescribable warmth as He begins to bring us to the place that we call "Spirit-filled". However, we need more than an occasional experience; we need to continue in the fullness of the Holy Spirit every hour of every day of our lives. To be "Spirit-filled", we must continue in union with Him through a continuing exchange of love with Him and with His family. Jesus described this as abiding in His love. Abiding in God's love is much more than knowing the occasional presence of the Holy Spirit - it is a continuing presence brought about by a continuing exchange of love - a giving and receiving of love with God and with each other. Simply put, if we abide in God's love, we have the fullness of His Holy Spirit. Of course, there is always a condition and that is we must truly make Jesus Lord of our lives - to have a heartfelt desire to obey His commandments. Jesus often talked about abiding in His love, but He always made it plain that we are dependent on Him and must learn to obey His commandments. He said, "If you love me, you will keep my commandments. And I will pray the Father and He will give you another counselor", the Holy Spirit. (John 14: 15-16).

Making Jesus Lord of our lives is not an option; it is a necessity if we are going to live the Christian life. It is so easy to claim His lordship and the fullness of His Holy Spirit, and convince ourselves that we belong to Him. But, the Bible is very clear about this; it says, "how can we be sure we belong to Him? By looking within ourselves:are we really trying to do what He wants us to? Some may say, "I am A Christian; I am on my way to heaven; I belong to Christ.' But if he doesn't do what Christ tells him to, he is a liar. But those who do what Christ tells them to will learn to love God more and more. That is the way to know whether or not you are a Christian." (1 John 2:3-5 LB). That is pretty straight talk right out of God's Word - to be a Christian is to obey God and abide in His love. There is no such thing as an undedicated Christian - the scripture says that if we are lukewarm, we will be rejected. There is no other way, we must love and obey, and if we do we will abide in God's love and know the fullness of His Holy Spirit. Let me give you exactly what Jesus said, "If you keep my commandments you will Abide in My love just as I have kept My Father's commandments and abide in His love." (John 15:10). If we obey, we abide in His love, and if we abide in His love, we have the abundance of a Spirit-filled life. The question then is: What did Jesus say about what we are commanded to do?

4
Commanded to Love

In the 22nd chapter of Matthew, Jesus was asked, "What is the most important command of God?" In answering Jesus drew together two fundamental commands of scripture, one from Deuteronomy 6:4 and the other from Leviticus 19:18. Here is what He said, "Love the Lord your God with all your heart, soul and mind.' This is the first and greatest commandment. The second most important is similar, 'Love your neighbor as much as you love yourself.' All the other commandments and all the demands of the prophets stem from these two laws and are fulfilled if you obey them. Keep only these and you will find you are obeying all the others." (Matthew 22:37-40 LB). In wedding these somewhat obscure commandments, Jesus reaffirmed them as His own, and in the process, gave us the scriptural principle that love fulfills or causes us to keep all the commandments of God. For instance, if you apply that kind of love to the Ten Commandments, you automatically keep them. If you love someone, how could you steal from him, or kill him, or take God's name in vain, or worship another god, and so on? Everything Jesus ever told us to do has to do with these two commands to love. However, He expanded them when He said, "A new commandment I give to you, that you love one another." (John 13:34 RSV). I believe He gave emphasis to this because in loving each other, we help each other to continue an exchange of love with God and our neighbors. So, with this statement, we can see just what His commandments are. Simply stated, the commandments of Jesus Christ are to love God, our neighbor, ourselves, and each other, not with just emotional love, but with God's kind of love. If we are to abide in God's love and live life more abundantly, we must dedicate our lives to the proposition that we will keep the commands of Jesus.

If you think about what Jesus has said, I think you will agree that to learn to love is the very reason for our being on this earth. How can we live with God, who is love, if we do not love Him and love those that He loves (our neighbor, ourselves, and each other)? How can we spend eternity in heaven, where love is the essence of everything, if we do not learn to love before we get there. We are on this earth, in these physical bodies to learn to keep Jesus' command to love. The more we love, the more we abide in God's love, that is, we have a more continuous exchange of love with Him, a continuing personal relationship. This is the very thing that goes on in heaven and the very reason that God created us in the first place. Because we are created in the likeness of God, we can enter into a personal relationship with Him and with others with the same kind of love that He continually offers to us.

Well, what kind of love does God have and what kind of love does He want us to have? Love in the Bible is more than the love people generally talk about. There is a special word for God's love in the original language of scripture, but in English, there is only the word love. This of course causes confusion, but Bible scholars agree that the love that Jesus was talking about was not romantic love or family love, it was "agape", the Greek word for Godly love. Godly love always wants to give and give; it is like an inexhaustible river that never stops flowing. God does not love us because of the qualities we have developed in ourselves - He loves us, because of what we can be in the union with Him as we abide in His love. Because we are made in His likeness, we have the capacity for His kind of life (spiritual life). When we receive it, we are commanded to love with His kind of love, a love that wants the very best for the one loved without any desire to get something in return. It is a love that seeks spiritual well-being for others, knowing that physical well-being will follow. It is a love that loves in spite of negative qualities in others. It is compassionate and offers mercy and forgiveness to everyone, even to those who make themselves an enemy. God's kind of love does not begin in the emotions where the self-life dominates, it begins in the will and causes the emotions to respond in the right way. If we are to live more abundantly, we must decide to love with God's kind of love, knowing that it will be possible only through the power that we receive, as we receive His love.

5
The Key To Loving God

The key to loving God, our neighbors, ourselves, and each other is to simply receive God's love. The scripture says that "God is love." (1 John 4:16). Therefore when we receive God's love, we receive Him and the power of His Holy Spirit. It is the power of the Holy Spirit that enables us to return God's love and obey the command to abide in His love. We have already seen that we must begin by receiving God's loving forgiveness. Now, we can go on to receive more of His love. Then, as we abide in His love, the fullness of His Holy Spirit makes it possible to return His love again and again in a continuing exchange of love. Many Christians try to love God without first receiving His love, but it is simply not possible. The scripture says, "We love God because He first loved us." (1 John 4:19). Because He loves us first, we can receive His love and the power to love, and go on to complete the exchange by loving Him in return. But, most of us try to love God without first receiving His love because it is easier to give than to receive. It takes real humility to truly receive a gift from others. Have you ever noticed that when someone gives us something, we sometimes want to give them something in return? On the surface, that is a good thing, but many times, our pride causes us to feel indebted to the giver, and we want to cancel the debt by giving them something in return. We need to realize that the gift represents the giver, that to truly receive the gift is to truly receive the giver. That is the way it is with the gift of God's love - if we humble ourselves and truly receive it, we will receive the giver, then He enables us to return His love. That is not canceling a debt - that is completing an exchange of love that, if continued, causes us to abide in Gods love and know the fullness of His Holy Spirit. Then the fullness of God's Holy Spirit produces abundance because our lives begin to bear fruit, the fruit of the Holy Spirit.

6
Abundance Means Much Fruit

The fruit of the Holy Spirit is love, joy, peace, patience, kindness, goodness, faithfulness, gentleness, and self-control." (Galatians 5:22-23). There is the abundance that Jesus promised us! Most people would settle for just the first three, love, joy and peace. But if you think about the other six on this list of spiritual fruit, I think you will agree that it includes absolutely everything we need to be successful in life. These are qualities that oil the gears of life. They make it possible to take advantage of our natural abilities and to have the right kind of relationships with others. Patience, for example, is necessary to learn how to make a living, or to be a good parent, or to develop athletic ability, or to just be a friend. There are hundreds of ways that these qualities can affect our lives for the better. They make us more effective in life and bring about the kind of relationships that create spiritual and material success. But, we cannot grow this fruit alone. Jesus said, "I am the vine, you are the branches. He who abides in me and I in him, he it is that bears much fruit, for apart from Me you can do nothing." (John 15:5). As long as we, the branches, abide or remain connected to Jesus, the Vine, we will bear much fruit. We have already seen that abiding in Jesus brings us the fullness and power of the Holy Spirit who is the source of this spiritual fruit. Now, we will see that it is His power that causes us to bear His fruit. One way that He does that is by equipping us to love through the use of special abilities that we call the gifts of the Holy Spirit. In the same passage that lists the fruit of the Holy Spirit, the scripture says: "If we live by the Spirit let us also walk by the Spirit." (Galatians 5:25). Walking by the Spirit, among other things, means that we must use the special abilities given to us by the Holy Spirit to minister to others with God's kind of love. There are many gifts of the Holy Spirit mentioned in the twelfth chapter of Romans, but each of us is given the special abilities we need to obey the command of Jesus to love God, our neighbor, ourselves, and each other. Through these gifts, such as teaching, serving, administration, and so on, we are given various practical ways of loving with God's kind of love. This, of course, benefits others, but the primary benefit is ours because the use of these gifts causes us to walk by the Spirit and obey the command of Jesus to love.

However, the gifts we receive are sometimes related to our natural abilities, and we are tempted to use them in our own strength. For instance, a school teacher that teaches a Bible class may not teach with "agape" love, but with only a human desire to be helpful or a desire to be looked up to by others. The teacher who abides in God's love and seeks to love his pupils with God's kind of love will know the power of the Holy Spirit and a teaching ability far beyond his natural ability. The added ability to teach is made possible by the activity of the Holy Spirit and part of that activity is the production of spiritual fruit like patience, gentleness, self-control, and so on. The Holy Spirit produces the spiritual fruit needed for the teacher to use the gift of teaching. Whatever our gifts or special abilities are, they are complemented by whatever fruit or special qualities that are needed. Then, the spiritual fruit that makes it possible to be a blessing to others, helps us to live more abundantly as we use those qualities to become more effective in other areas of life. That same Bible teacher will become a better school teacher and better able to teach his own children. Then, life becomes more and more fulfilling as the fruit of the Holy Spirit makes him more and more effective in everything he does. We always reap what we sow; when we are a blessing to others, we are blessed ourselves. When we are ministering to the needs of others with the gifts of the Holy Spirit, everyone concerned is blessed because God's kind of love is being exchanged with our neighbor and each other. This love is the first of the fruit of the Holy Spirit listed in scripture, and I believe the reason is that the Holy Spirit will produce the other fruit only as we obey the command of Jesus to love and abide in His love. As we abide in His love, a measure of joy and peace appears. Then as we continue to abide or continue in that exchange of love, we willingly allow the gifts of the Holy Spirit to operate - then various other fruit appear, and we begin to bear much fruit. That is, we become joyful, peaceful, patient, kind, good, faithful, gentle, and self-controlled - the qualities that enable us to live more abundantly.

I believe that any Christian who seriously looks at life will agree that Jesus offers us abundance beyond what we would ever "ask or think." Most of us receive a very small portion of that abundance simply because we are not willing to accept it. Most of us would say that just living this physical life is distracting, or that we have to be preoccupied with life to maintain a certain life-style. But, when I looked at my own life, I knew that, that was not it at all. There is one reason that I do not have more abundance and that is, I am not willing to receive it. In the past, I have been convinced that these things were for somebody more spiritual than I, or for people that had more time to be spiritual - or anything that seemed to get me off the hook. But, I know that thinking was not from God - it was right out of the pit of hell. I know now that I was not willing to receive the things from God that would have given me a more abundant life because I was not willing to be submissive enough to accept them. We have seen that it takes humility to truly receive a gift, but to receive life-changing gifts from God, it takes more - it takes submission.

If we are to receive the gifts from God that lead to abundance, we must submit ourselves to His wisdom and His control. Without that we will not be able to receive the gifts of the Holy Spirit that make it possible to "bear much fruit". It goes without saying that fruit is always borne on branches. Since Jesus is the vine and we are the branches, we must submit ourselves to Him in the same way that a branch submits to the vine, totally and without reservation.

The problem is that the human mind can devise all kinds of ways to convince us that we are submissive. The most common is substituting something for submission. For instance, many Christians become serious Bible students thinking that study in itself is submission. They submit to God's word without submitting to God personally. It is possible to gain knowledge about God's word and believe it and still not receive the abundance it offers. We must abide in God's love to receive from Him, and that takes submission of the entire personality. We cannot read the Bible decide what we need, when we need it, and then expect God to give it to us. That is not what a branch does. The branch knows that it will receive exactly what it needs, when it needs it, as long as it abides or remains submitted to the vine in a continuing exchange of nutrients. when we abide in Jesus, the Vine, through the same kind of submission, we get what we pray for. Here is what Jesus said. "If you abide in Me and My words abide in you, you will ask what you desire, and it will be done for you." (John 15:7). If we submit ourselves to the point that we are abiding (having a continuous exchange of love), we begin to recognize the importance of spiritual fruit. Then, we know what to ask for because we are led by the Holy Spirit to ask for what every branch desires - fruit. As we receive the fruit of the Holy Spirit, we become normal, healthy Christians.

7
Normal Christian Life

What we are talking about is the normal Christian life. A Christian that is not developing the qualities, called the fruit of the Holy Spirit, is a sick Christian. There is no such thing as a nominal or marginal Christian. If we are not normal fruit-bearing Christians, we are either sick and back-slidden or we are not Christians at all. There is absolutely nothing in the scripture to justify the idea that some people are nominal Christians. Jesus was very explicit about that. He said, "Because you are lukewarm and neither cold nor hot, I will spew you out of my mouth." (Revelation 3:16). "Spew" was a figurative term used to show His complete incompatibility with anyone that was not willing to submit their entire life to Him. Incompatibility eliminates any possibility of abiding in Jesus' love, any possibility of bearing fruit, and any possibility of living more abundantly. If we are not bearing more and more fruit and living more abundantly year by year, it means one thing - we are unwilling to be submissive enough to receive the things God wants to give us.

It is my hope that you have found yourself to be a submissive fruit-bearing Christian. In my life, I have experienced the misery of knowing about the abundance that God has for us without receiving it. I was spiritually sick without being conscious of it - so much so that, at one point, I was convinced that I was bearing much fruit, when in reality I was a branch that was altogether barren of fruit. If God has shown you a need for fruit in your life, I hope you will do as I am doing - seeking to receive the healing love of the Great Physician. Begin by receiving His loving forgiveness and go on to continually exchange love with Him in the greatest relationship you will ever know - a relationship that will accomplish God's purpose in this life and the life to come. We have such a short time in this life to be prepared to live with our heavenly Father - let us make the most of the time we have. Let us live more abundantly now so that we will live more abundantly in eternity.

NOTES

NOTES

NOTES